The *Ultimate* HAPPINESS *Journal*

Experiencing Daily Joy

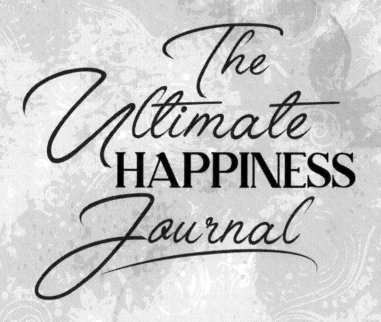

The Ultimate HAPPINESS Journal

This Journal Belongs To

_____

Created by Umair Qureshi & Beth Jarboe-Elkassih

Copyright © 2019 Zulzan LLC.

The Ultimate HAPPINESS Journal

Are you ready to begin your 90 day journey to living the best life you deserve to be living? 90 days is a perfect length of time to reap a new habit, a lifestyle change or an attitude shift towards daily happiness. Live your most intentional life. Set meaningful goals. Determine your happiest moments, determine how grateful you are and journal your daily greatest achievements.

You can record your moments of happiness and gratitude each day. This Ultimate Happiness Journal is designed so you can shift your mental well-being into one of habitual joy and positivity in your daily life.

You will be creating new and improved 'habits' of gratitude and a lifestyle shift in focusing on the good every day. Each day a new inspiring and motivational quote will set the tone to get thru your day.

After consistently journaling for 90 days (approximately 13 weeks), you will literally see and feel your attitude toward life change. You WILL be happier, you WILL be able to see the 'good' in everyday events and you WILL be able to move forward towards living a more positive and fulfilled life of joy, love and happiness.

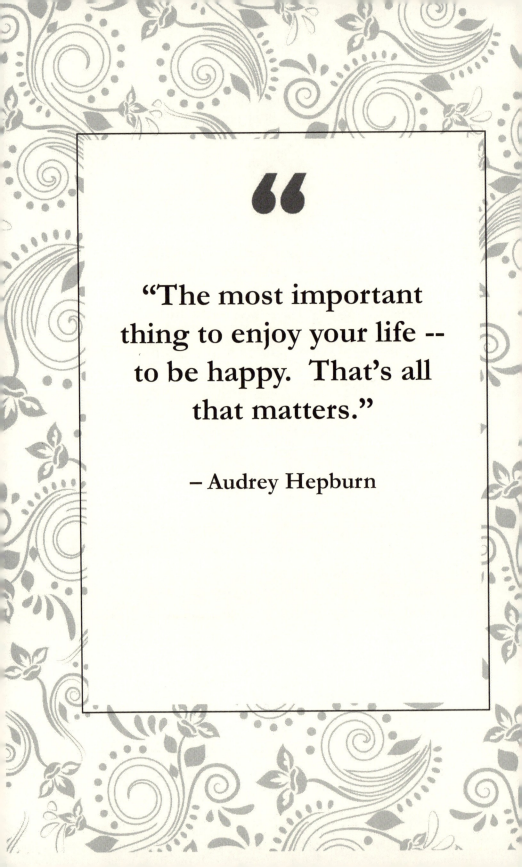

"The most important thing to enjoy your life -- to be happy. That's all that matters."

– Audrey Hepburn

THE ULTIMATE HAPPINESS JOURNAL

Date: _____

Today's Happiest Moments:

_____
_____
_____

- ☐ Today I smiled at least once to a stranger.
- ☐ Today I did an intentional act of kindness.
- ☐ Today I spent at least 15+ minutes reading inspirational content of my choice.

3 Things I'm Most Grateful For:

_____
_____
_____

What Could I Have Done Better?

_____
_____
_____

Goals/Plans for Tomorrow:

_____
_____
_____

Today's Great Accomplishments:

_____
_____
_____

How Happy Are You Feeling?

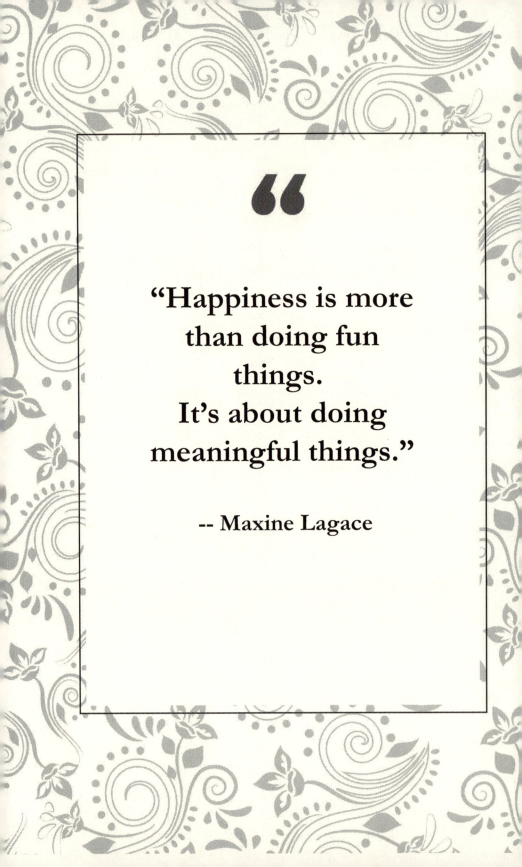

"

"Happiness is more than doing fun things.
It's about doing meaningful things."

-- Maxine Lagace

THE ULTIMATE HAPPINESS JOURNAL

Date: _____

Today's Happiest Moments:

_____
_____
_____

☐ Today I smiled at least once to a stranger.
☐ Today I did an intentional act of kindness.
☐ Today I spent at least 15+ minutes reading
inspirational content of my choice.

3 Things I'm Most Grateful For:

_____
_____
_____

What Could I Have Done Better?

_____
_____
_____

Goals/Plans for Tomorrow:

_____
_____
_____

Today's Great Accomplishments:

_____
_____
_____

How Happy Are You Feeling?

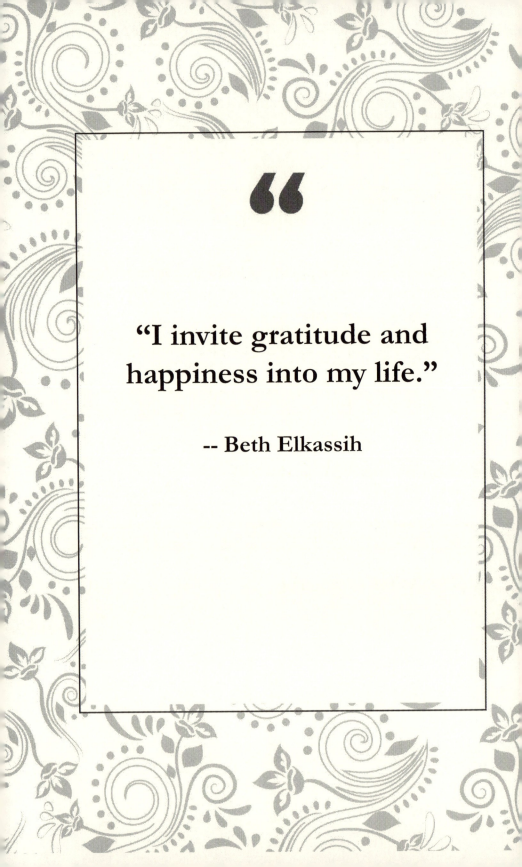

"

"I invite gratitude and happiness into my life."

-- Beth Elkassih

THE ULTIMATE HAPPINESS JOURNAL

Date: _____

Today's Happiest Moments:

_____
_____
_____

☐ Today I smiled at least once to a stranger.
☐ Today I did an intentional act of kindness.
☐ Today I spent at least 15+ minutes reading
inspirational content of my choice.

3 Things I'm Most Grateful For:

_____
_____
_____

What Could I Have Done Better?

_____
_____
_____

Goals/Plans for Tomorrow:

_____
_____
_____

Today's Great Accomplishments:

_____
_____
_____

How Happy Are You Feeling?   ☺ 😐 ☹

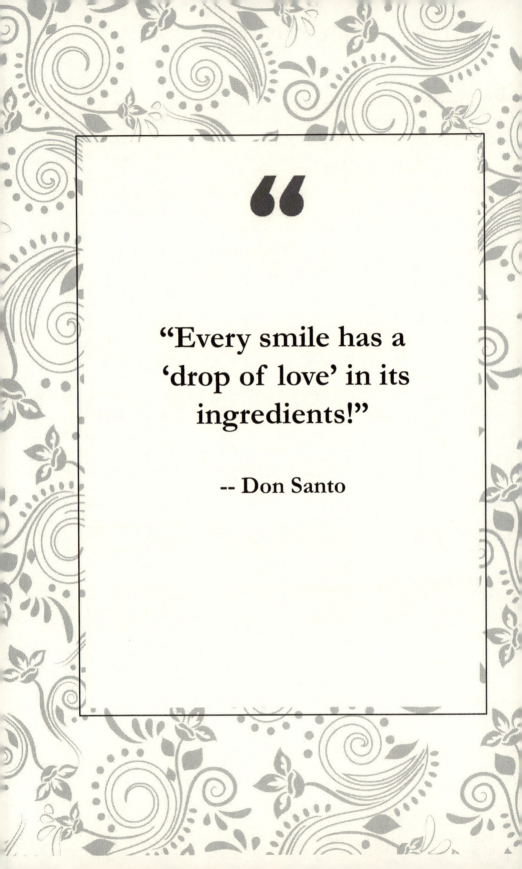

"

"Every smile has a 'drop of love' in its ingredients!"

-- Don Santo

THE ULTIMATE HAPPINESS JOURNAL

Date: _____

Today's Happiest Moments:

_____
_____
_____

☐ Today I smiled at least once to a stranger.
☐ Today I did an intentional act of kindness.
☐ Today I spent at least 15+ minutes reading
inspirational content of my choice.

3 Things I'm Most Grateful For:

_____
_____
_____

What Could I Have Done Better?

_____
_____
_____

Goals/Plans for Tomorrow:

_____
_____
_____

Today's Great Accomplishments:

_____
_____
_____

How Happy Are You Feeling?

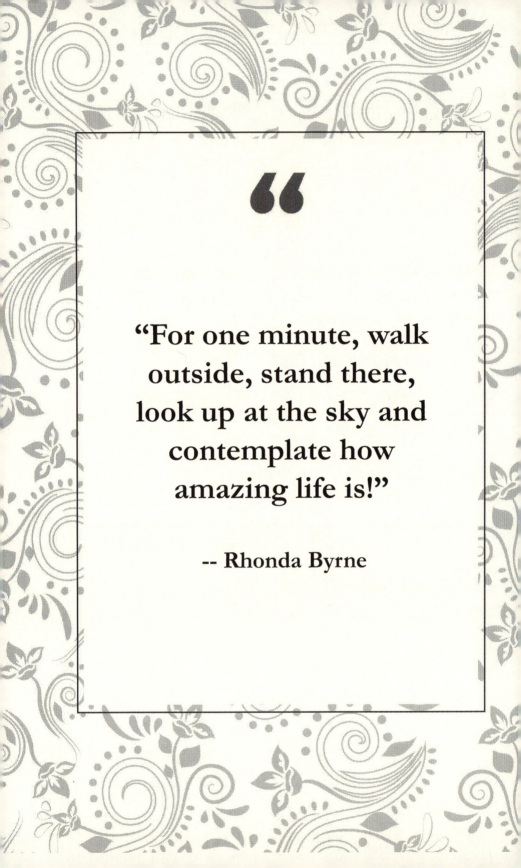

"For one minute, walk outside, stand there, look up at the sky and contemplate how amazing life is!"

-- Rhonda Byrne

THE ULTIMATE HAPPINESS JOURNAL

Date: _____

Today's Happiest Moments:

_____

_____

_____

☐ Today I smiled at least once to a stranger.
☐ Today I did an intentional act of kindness.
☐ Today I spent at least 15+ minutes reading
inspirational content of my choice.

3 Things I'm Most Grateful For:

_____

_____

_____

What Could I Have Done Better?

_____

_____

_____

Goals/Plans for Tomorrow:

_____

_____

_____

Today's Great Accomplishments:

_____

_____

_____

How Happy Are You Feeling?

"**Protect your joy. Don't let anyone take it away from you. It's yours!**"

-- Beth Elkassih

THE ULTIMATE HAPPINESS JOURNAL

Date: _____

Today's Happiest Moments:

_____
_____
_____

☐ Today I smiled at least once to a stranger.
☐ Today I did an intentional act of kindness.
☐ Today I spent at least 15+ minutes reading inspirational content of my choice.

3 Things I'm Most Grateful For:

_____
_____
_____

What Could I Have Done Better?

_____
_____
_____

Goals/Plans for Tomorrow:

_____
_____
_____

Today's Great Accomplishments:

_____
_____
_____

How Happy Are You Feeling?   ☹

66

"The more we care for
the happiness of others,
the greater our own
sense of well-being." –

Dalai Lama

THE ULTIMATE HAPPINESS JOURNAL

Date: _____

Today's Happiest Moments:

_____
_____
_____

- ☐ Today I smiled at least once to a stranger.
- ☐ Today I did an intentional act of kindness.
- ☐ Today I spent at least 15+ minutes reading inspirational content of my choice.

3 Things I'm Most Grateful For:

_____
_____
_____

What Could I Have Done Better?

_____
_____
_____

Goals/Plans for Tomorrow:

_____
_____
_____

Today's Great Accomplishments:

_____
_____
_____

How Happy Are You Feeling?   ☺ ☺ ☹

"

"Good humor is a tonic
for mind and body. It
simply makes you
happy."

-- Beth Elkassih

THE ULTIMATE HAPPINESS JOURNAL

Date: _____

Today's Happiest Moments:

_____
_____
_____

☐ Today I smiled at least once to a stranger.
☐ Today I did an intentional act of kindness.
☐ Today I spent at least 15+ minutes reading
inspirational content of my choice.

3 Things I'm Most Grateful For:

_____
_____
_____

What Could I Have Done Better?

_____
_____
_____

Goals/Plans for Tomorrow:

_____
_____
_____

Today's Great Accomplishments:

_____
_____
_____

How Happy Are You Feeling?   ☺   😐   ☹

"There's nothing wrong in being silly once in awhile!"

-- Beth Elkassih

THE ULTIMATE HAPPINESS JOURNAL

Date: _____

Today's Happiest Moments:

_____
_____
_____

☐ Today I smiled at least once to a stranger.
☐ Today I did an intentional act of kindness.
☐ Today I spent at least 15+ minutes reading
inspirational content of my choice.

3 Things I'm Most Grateful For:

_____
_____
_____

What Could I Have Done Better?

_____
_____
_____

Goals/Plans for Tomorrow:

_____
_____
_____

Today's Great Accomplishments:

_____
_____
_____

How Happy Are You Feeling?   ☺ 😐 ☹

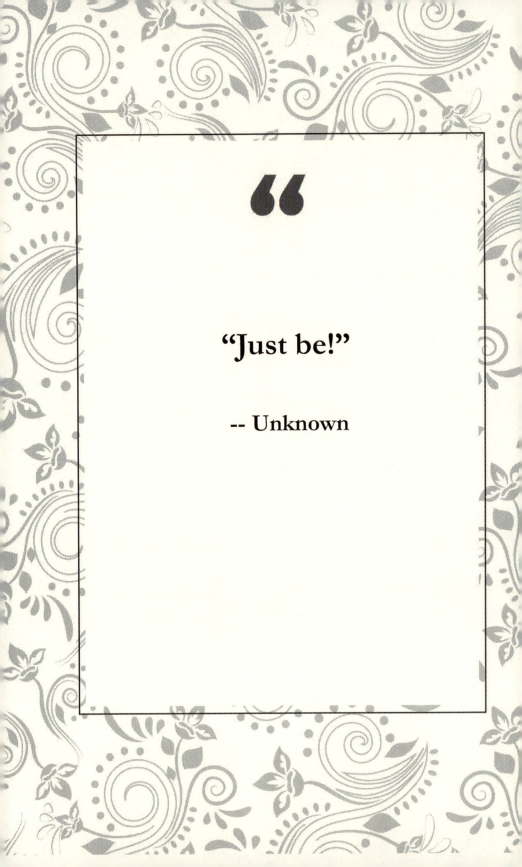

"Just be!"

-- Unknown

THE ULTIMATE HAPPINESS JOURNAL

Date: _____

Today's Happiest Moments:

_____
_____
_____

☐ Today I smiled at least once to a stranger.
☐ Today I did an intentional act of kindness.
☐ Today I spent at least 15+ minutes reading
inspirational content of my choice.

3 Things I'm Most Grateful For:

_____
_____
_____

What Could I Have Done Better?

_____
_____
_____

Goals/Plans for Tomorrow:

_____
_____
_____

Today's Great Accomplishments:

_____
_____
_____

How Happy Are You Feeling?

"Having happy friends
can and will make you
happy."

-- Beth Elkassih

THE ULTIMATE HAPPINESS JOURNAL

Date: _____

Today's Happiest Moments:

_____
_____
_____

☐ Today I smiled at least once to a stranger.
☐ Today I did an intentional act of kindness.
☐ Today I spent at least 15+ minutes reading inspirational content of my choice.

3 Things I'm Most Grateful For:

_____
_____
_____

What Could I Have Done Better?

_____
_____
_____

Goals/Plans for Tomorrow:

_____
_____
_____

Today's Great Accomplishments:

_____
_____
_____

How Happy Are You Feeling?　　☺　☺　☹

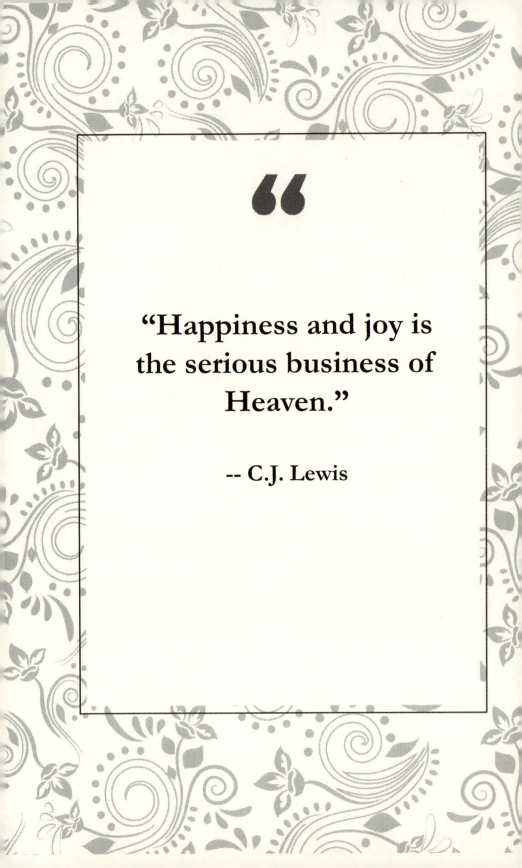

"Happiness and joy is the serious business of Heaven."

-- C.J. Lewis

THE ULTIMATE HAPPINESS JOURNAL

Date: _____

Today's Happiest Moments:

_____
_____
_____

☐ Today I smiled at least once to a stranger.
☐ Today I did an intentional act of kindness.
☐ Today I spent at least 15+ minutes reading
inspirational content of my choice.

3 Things I'm Most Grateful For:

_____
_____
_____

What Could I Have Done Better?

_____
_____
_____

Goals/Plans for Tomorrow:

_____
_____
_____

Today's Great Accomplishments:

_____
_____
_____

How Happy Are You Feeling?   ☺ 😐 ☹

"If you can't be the sunshine, then BE the sunshine!"

-- Fatima Karim

THE ULTIMATE HAPPINESS JOURNAL

Date: _____

Today's Happiest Moments:

_____
_____
_____

- ☐ Today I smiled at least once to a stranger.
- ☐ Today I did an intentional act of kindness.
- ☐ Today I spent at least 15+ minutes reading inspirational content of my choice.

3 Things I'm Most Grateful For:

_____
_____
_____

What Could I Have Done Better?

_____
_____
_____

Goals/Plans for Tomorrow:

_____
_____
_____

Today's Great Accomplishments:

_____
_____
_____

How Happy Are You Feeling?

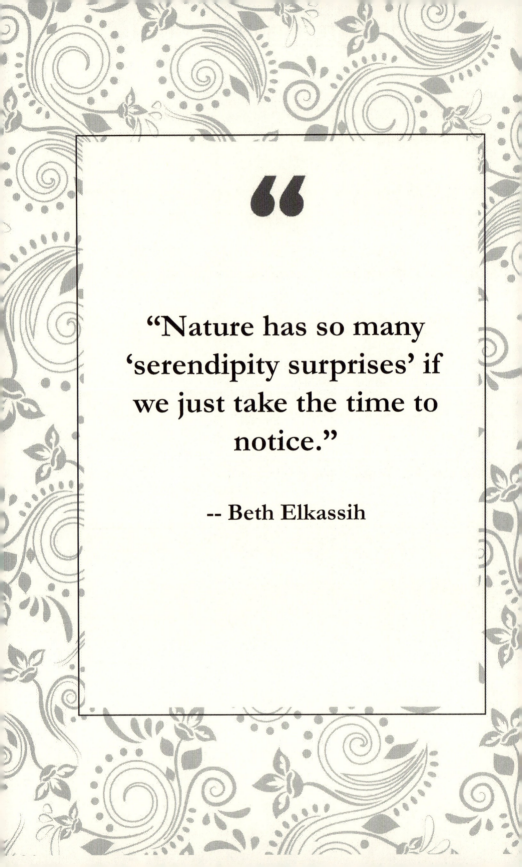

"Nature has so many 'serendipity surprises' if we just take the time to notice."

-- Beth Elkassih

THE ULTIMATE HAPPINESS JOURNAL

Date: _____

Today's Happiest Moments:

_____
_____
_____

☐ Today I smiled at least once to a stranger.
☐ Today I did an intentional act of kindness.
☐ Today I spent at least 15+ minutes reading
inspirational content of my choice.

3 Things I'm Most Grateful For:

_____
_____
_____

What Could I Have Done Better?

_____
_____
_____

Goals/Plans for Tomorrow:

_____
_____
_____

Today's Great Accomplishments:

_____
_____
_____

How Happy Are You Feeling?   ☺   😐   ☹

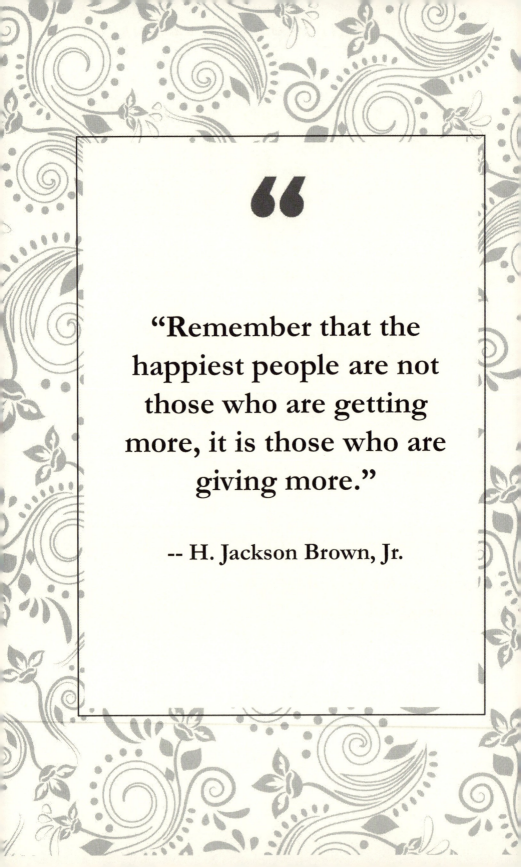

"Remember that the happiest people are not those who are getting more, it is those who are giving more."

-- H. Jackson Brown, Jr.

THE ULTIMATE HAPPINESS JOURNAL

Date: _____

Today's Happiest Moments:

_____

_____

_____

☐ Today I smiled at least once to a stranger.
☐ Today I did an intentional act of kindness.
☐ Today I spent at least 15+ minutes reading
inspirational content of my choice.

3 Things I'm Most Grateful For:

_____

_____

_____

What Could I Have Done Better?

_____

_____

_____

Goals/Plans for Tomorrow:

_____

_____

_____

Today's Great Accomplishments:

_____

_____

_____

How Happy Are You Feeling?

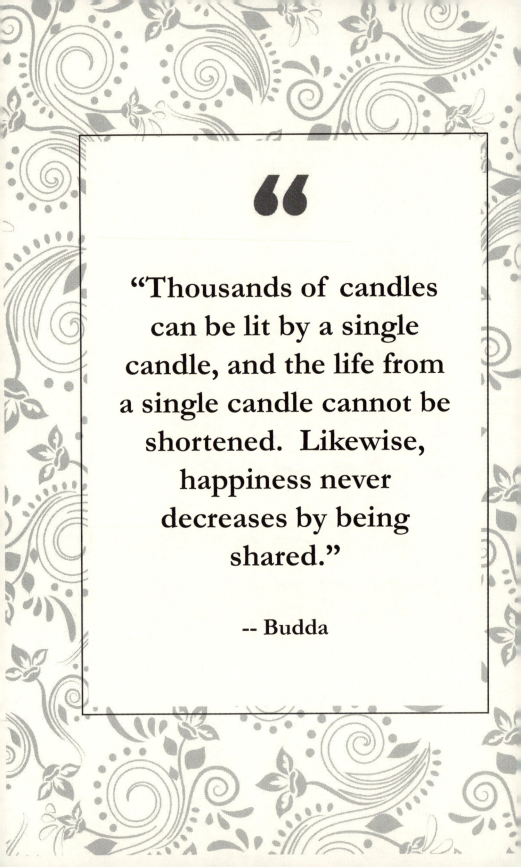

"

"Thousands of candles can be lit by a single candle, and the life from a single candle cannot be shortened. Likewise, happiness never decreases by being shared."

-- Budda

THE ULTIMATE HAPPINESS JOURNAL

Date: _____

Today's Happiest Moments:

_____
_____
_____

- ☐ Today I smiled at least once to a stranger.
- ☐ Today I did an intentional act of kindness.
- ☐ Today I spent at least 15+ minutes reading inspirational content of my choice.

3 Things I'm Most Grateful For:

_____
_____
_____

What Could I Have Done Better?

_____
_____
_____

Goals/Plans for Tomorrow:

_____
_____
_____

Today's Great Accomplishments:

_____
_____
_____

How Happy Are You Feeling?

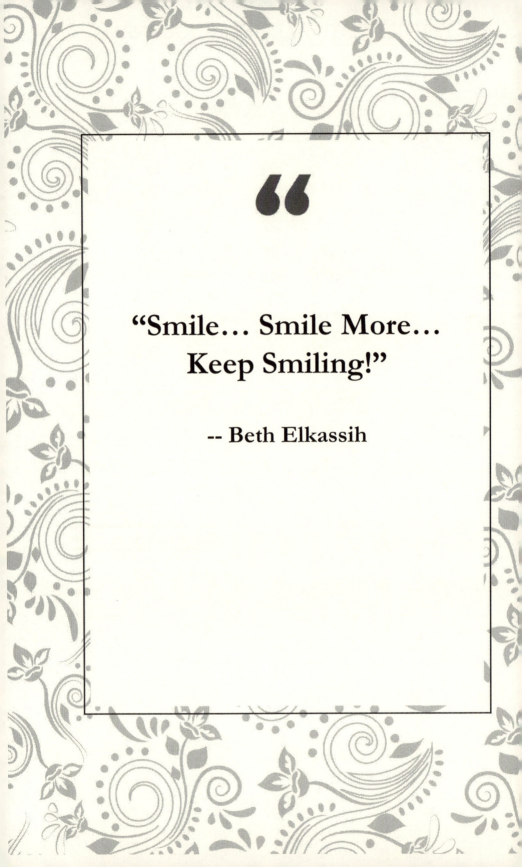

"

"Smile… Smile More… Keep Smiling!"

-- Beth Elkassih

THE ULTIMATE HAPPINESS JOURNAL

Date: _____

Today's Happiest Moments:

_____

_____

_____

☐ Today I smiled at least once to a stranger.
☐ Today I did an intentional act of kindness.
☐ Today I spent at least 15+ minutes reading inspirational content of my choice.

3 Things I'm Most Grateful For:

_____

_____

_____

What Could I Have Done Better?

_____

_____

_____

Goals/Plans for Tomorrow:

_____

_____

_____

Today's Great Accomplishments:

_____

_____

_____

How Happy Are You Feeling?   ☺ 😐 ☹

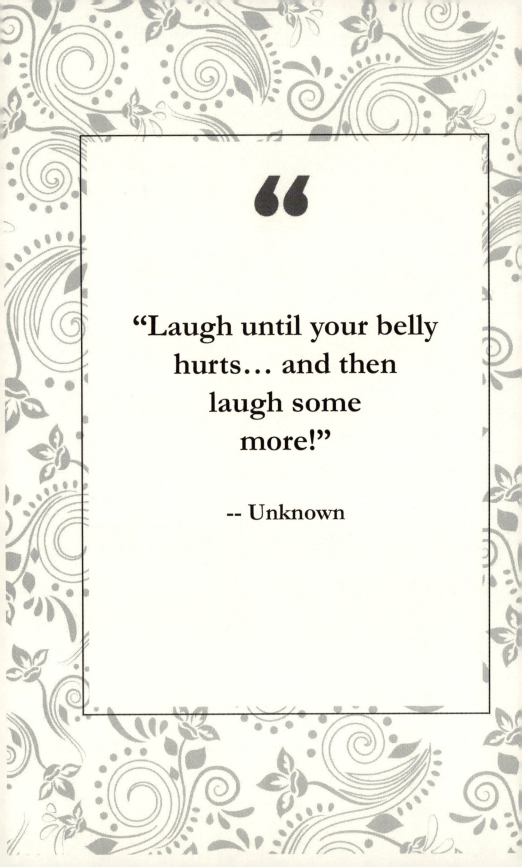

66

"Laugh until your belly hurts… and then laugh some more!"

-- Unknown

THE ULTIMATE HAPPINESS JOURNAL

Date: _____

Today's Happiest Moments:

_____

_____

_____

☐ Today I smiled at least once to a stranger.
☐ Today I did an intentional act of kindness.
☐ Today I spent at least 15+ minutes reading inspirational content of my choice.

3 Things I'm Most Grateful For:

_____

_____

_____

What Could I Have Done Better?

_____

_____

_____

Goals/Plans for Tomorrow:

_____

_____

_____

Today's Great Accomplishments:

_____

_____

_____

How Happy Are You Feeling?   ☺ 😐 ☹

"If you have only one smile to give, then give it one you love."

-- Maya Angelou

THE ULTIMATE HAPPINESS JOURNAL

Date: _____

Today's Happiest Moments:

_____
_____
_____

- ☐ Today I smiled at least once to a stranger.
- ☐ Today I did an intentional act of kindness.
- ☐ Today I spent at least 15+ minutes reading inspirational content of my choice.

3 Things I'm Most Grateful For:

_____
_____
_____

What Could I Have Done Better?

_____
_____
_____

Goals/Plans for Tomorrow:

_____
_____
_____

Today's Great Accomplishments:

_____
_____
_____

How Happy Are You Feeling?   ☺ 😐 ☹

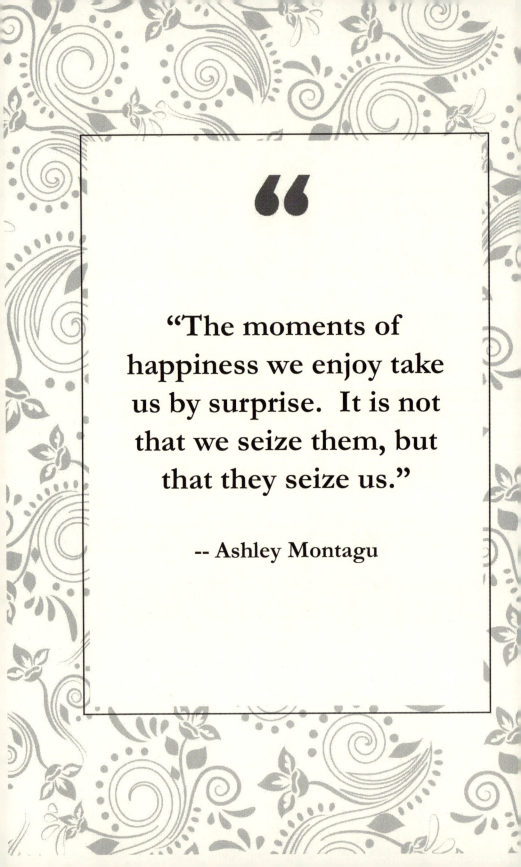

"The moments of happiness we enjoy take us by surprise. It is not that we seize them, but that they seize us."

-- Ashley Montagu

THE ULTIMATE HAPPINESS JOURNAL

Date: _____

Today's Happiest Moments:

_____
_____
_____

☐ Today I smiled at least once to a stranger.
☐ Today I did an intentional act of kindness.
☐ Today I spent at least 15+ minutes reading
inspirational content of my choice.

3 Things I'm Most Grateful For:

_____
_____
_____

What Could I Have Done Better?

_____
_____
_____

Goals/Plans for Tomorrow:

_____
_____
_____

Today's Great Accomplishments:

_____
_____
_____

How Happy Are You Feeling?   ☺ ☻ ☹

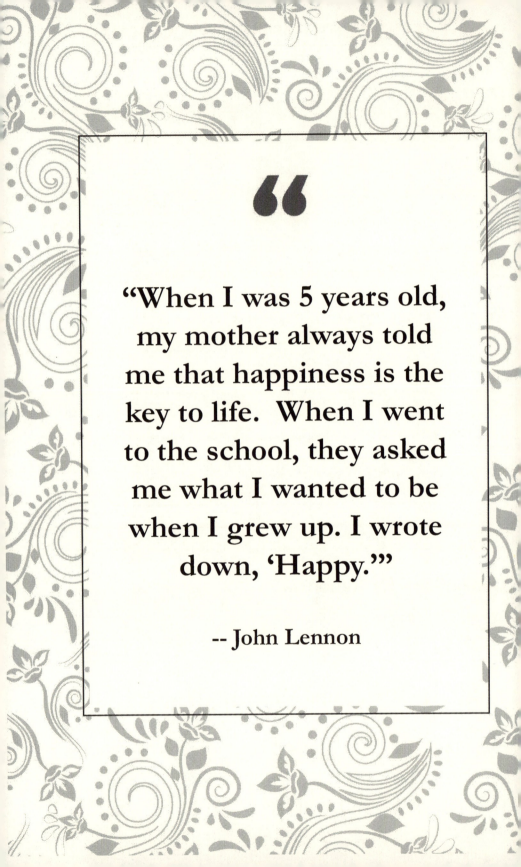

"When I was 5 years old, my mother always told me that happiness is the key to life. When I went to the school, they asked me what I wanted to be when I grew up. I wrote down, 'Happy.'"

-- John Lennon

THE ULTIMATE HAPPINESS JOURNAL

Date: _____

Today's Happiest Moments:

_____
_____
_____

☐ Today I smiled at least once to a stranger.
☐ Today I did an intentional act of kindness.
☐ Today I spent at least 15+ minutes reading
inspirational content of my choice.

3 Things I'm Most Grateful For:

_____
_____
_____

What Could I Have Done Better?

_____
_____
_____

Goals/Plans for Tomorrow:

_____
_____
_____

Today's Great Accomplishments:

_____
_____
_____

How Happy Are You Feeling?   ☺ ☺ ☹

"

"If you smile when no one else is around… then you are truly happy."

-- Andy Rooney

THE ULTIMATE HAPPINESS JOURNAL

Date: _____

Today's Happiest Moments:

_____

_____

_____

☐ Today I smiled at least once to a stranger.
☐ Today I did an intentional act of kindness.
☐ Today I spent at least 15+ minutes reading
inspirational content of my choice.

3 Things I'm Most Grateful For:

_____

_____

_____

What Could I Have Done Better?

_____

_____

_____

Goals/Plans for Tomorrow:

_____

_____

_____

Today's Great Accomplishments:

_____

_____

_____

How Happy Are You Feeling?   ☺ 😐 ☹

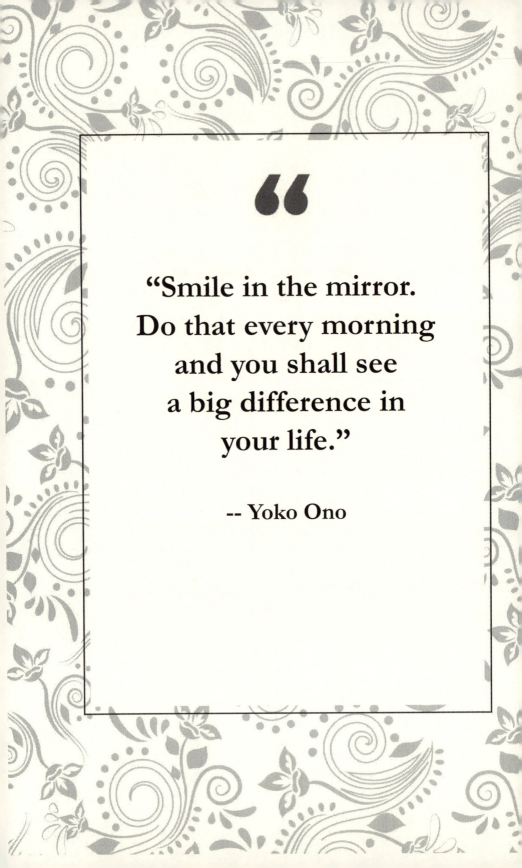

"Smile in the mirror.
Do that every morning
and you shall see
a big difference in
your life."

-- Yoko Ono

THE ULTIMATE HAPPINESS JOURNAL

Date: _____

Today's Happiest Moments:

_____

_____

_____

☐ Today I smiled at least once to a stranger.
☐ Today I did an intentional act of kindness.
☐ Today I spent at least 15+ minutes reading inspirational content of my choice.

3 Things I'm Most Grateful For:

_____

_____

_____

What Could I Have Done Better?

_____

_____

_____

Goals/Plans for Tomorrow:

_____

_____

_____

Today's Great Accomplishments:

_____

_____

_____

How Happy Are You Feeling?   ☺   ☺   ☹

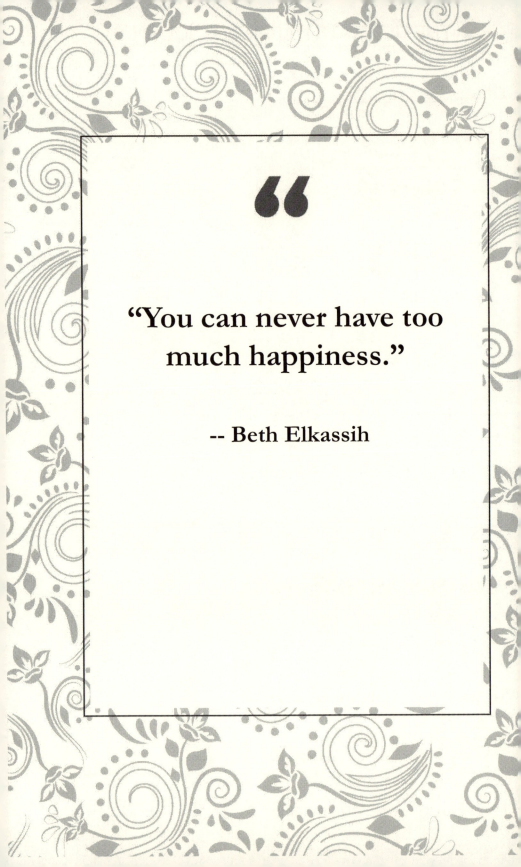

"You can never have too much happiness."

-- Beth Elkassih

THE ULTIMATE HAPPINESS JOURNAL

Date: _____

Today's Happiest Moments:

_____
_____
_____

☐ Today I smiled at least once to a stranger.
☐ Today I did an intentional act of kindness.
☐ Today I spent at least 15+ minutes reading
inspirational content of my choice.

3 Things I'm Most Grateful For:

_____
_____
_____

What Could I Have Done Better?

_____
_____
_____

Goals/Plans for Tomorrow:

_____
_____
_____

Today's Great Accomplishments:

_____
_____
_____

How Happy Are You Feeling?   ☺ ☺ ☹

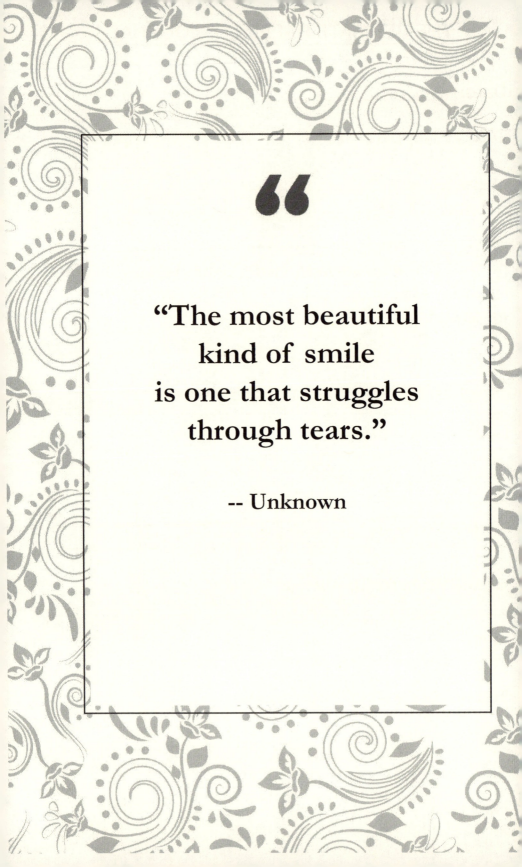

**"The most beautiful
kind of smile
is one that struggles
through tears."**

-- Unknown

THE ULTIMATE HAPPINESS JOURNAL

Date: _____

Today's Happiest Moments:

_____

_____

_____

☐ Today I smiled at least once to a stranger.
☐ Today I did an intentional act of kindness.
☐ Today I spent at least 15+ minutes reading inspirational content of my choice.

3 Things I'm Most Grateful For:

_____

_____

_____

What Could I Have Done Better?

_____

_____

_____

Goals/Plans for Tomorrow:

_____

_____

_____

Today's Great Accomplishments:

_____

_____

_____

How Happy Are You Feeling?

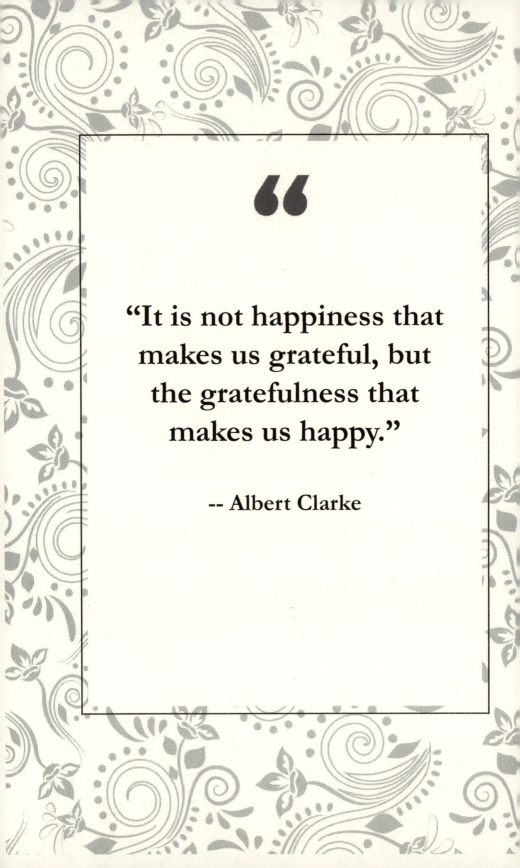

66

"It is not happiness that
makes us grateful, but
the gratefulness that
makes us happy."

-- Albert Clarke

THE ULTIMATE HAPPINESS JOURNAL

Date: _____

Today's Happiest Moments:

_____
_____
_____

☐ Today I smiled at least once to a stranger.
☐ Today I did an intentional act of kindness.
☐ Today I spent at least 15+ minutes reading
inspirational content of my choice.

3 Things I'm Most Grateful For:

_____
_____
_____

What Could I Have Done Better?

_____
_____
_____

Goals/Plans for Tomorrow:

_____
_____
_____

Today's Great Accomplishments:

_____
_____
_____

How Happy Are You Feeling?

"Imagine all the good that a simple smile will do!."

-- Beth Elkassih

THE ULTIMATE HAPPINESS JOURNAL

Date: _____

Today's Happiest Moments:

_____
_____
_____

☐ Today I smiled at least once to a stranger.
☐ Today I did an intentional act of kindness.
☐ Today I spent at least 15+ minutes reading
inspirational content of my choice.

3 Things I'm Most Grateful For:

_____
_____
_____

What Could I Have Done Better?

_____
_____
_____

Goals/Plans for Tomorrow:

_____
_____
_____

Today's Great Accomplishments:

_____
_____
_____

How Happy Are You Feeling?   ☺ ☺ ☹

"**Sometimes your joy is the source of your smile, but sometimes your smile is the source of your joy and happiness.**"

-- Thich Hanh

THE ULTIMATE HAPPINESS JOURNAL

Date: _____

Today's Happiest Moments:

_____
_____
_____

☐ Today I smiled at least once to a stranger.
☐ Today I did an intentional act of kindness.
☐ Today I spent at least 15+ minutes reading
inspirational content of my choice.

3 Things I'm Most Grateful For:

_____
_____
_____

What Could I Have Done Better?

_____
_____
_____

Goals/Plans for Tomorrow:

_____
_____
_____

Today's Great Accomplishments:

_____
_____
_____

How Happy Are You Feeling?   ☺   ☻   ☹

66

"We don't laugh because we are happy. We are happy because we laugh."

-- William James

THE ULTIMATE HAPPINESS JOURNAL

Date: _____

Today's Happiest Moments:

_____
_____
_____

- ☐ Today I smiled at least once to a stranger.
- ☐ Today I did an intentional act of kindness.
- ☐ Today I spent at least 15+ minutes reading inspirational content of my choice.

3 Things I'm Most Grateful For:

_____
_____
_____

What Could I Have Done Better?

_____
_____
_____

Goals/Plans for Tomorrow:

_____
_____
_____

Today's Great Accomplishments:

_____
_____
_____

How Happy Are You Feeling?   ☺ 😐 ☹

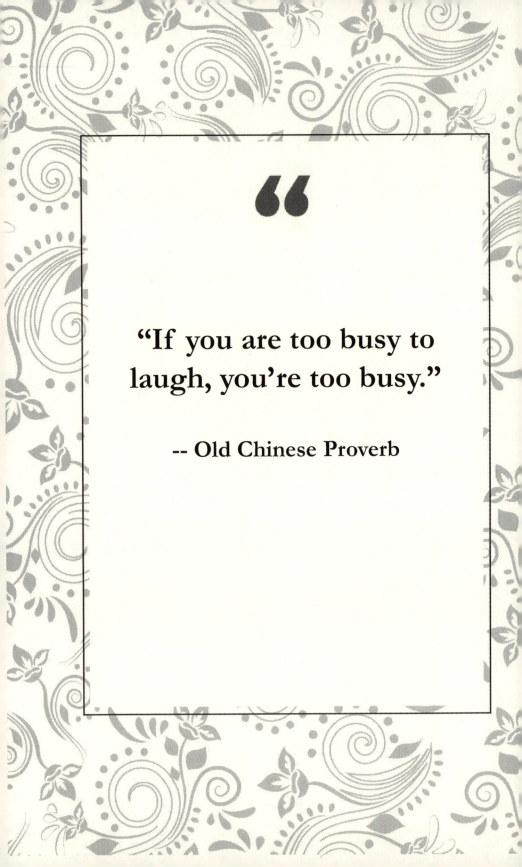

"If you are too busy to laugh, you're too busy."

-- Old Chinese Proverb

THE ULTIMATE HAPPINESS JOURNAL

Date: _____

Today's Happiest Moments:

_____

_____

_____

☐ Today I smiled at least once to a stranger.
☐ Today I did an intentional act of kindness.
☐ Today I spent at least 15+ minutes reading
inspirational content of my choice.

3 Things I'm Most Grateful For:

_____

_____

_____

What Could I Have Done Better?

_____

_____

_____

Goals/Plans for Tomorrow:

_____

_____

_____

Today's Great Accomplishments:

_____

_____

_____

How Happy Are You Feeling?   ☺ 😐 ☹

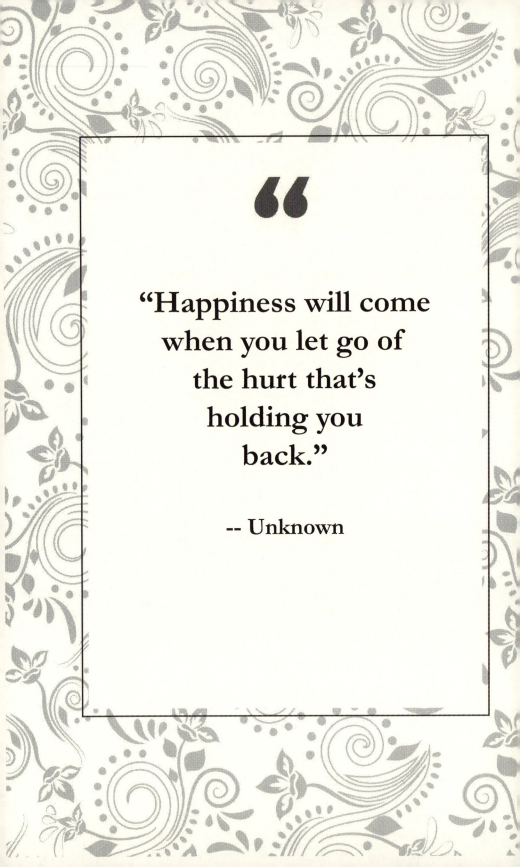

"**Happiness will come when you let go of the hurt that's holding you back.**"

-- Unknown

30 DAY REFLECTIONS

Congratulations in completing the first 30 days of your 90-day Happiness journey. Let's take time out and reflect upon the past month.

How fulfilling has been the past 30 days/month?

_____
_____
_____

Did you achieve any of your weekly or monthly goals, and if so, what were they and what did you learn?

_____
_____
_____

Is there anything you would have done differently?

_____
_____
_____

What was the most enjoyable activity or activities you experienced these last 30 days?

_____
_____
_____

What is your most memorable 'act of kindness' you did for someone and one you received from someone?

_____
_____
_____

Name 3 Goals and/or Habits you wish to master for the next 30 days:

_____
_____
_____

66

"Don't look for happiness. CREATE it!"

-- Beth Elkassih

THE ULTIMATE HAPPINESS JOURNAL

Date: _____

Today's Happiest Moments:

_____
_____
_____

☐ Today I smiled at least once to a stranger.
☐ Today I did an intentional act of kindness.
☐ Today I spent at least 15+ minutes reading
inspirational content of my choice.

3 Things I'm Most Grateful For:

_____
_____
_____

What Could I Have Done Better?

_____
_____
_____

Goals/Plans for Tomorrow:

_____
_____
_____

Today's Great Accomplishments:

_____
_____
_____

How Happy Are You Feeling?   ☺ 😐 ☹

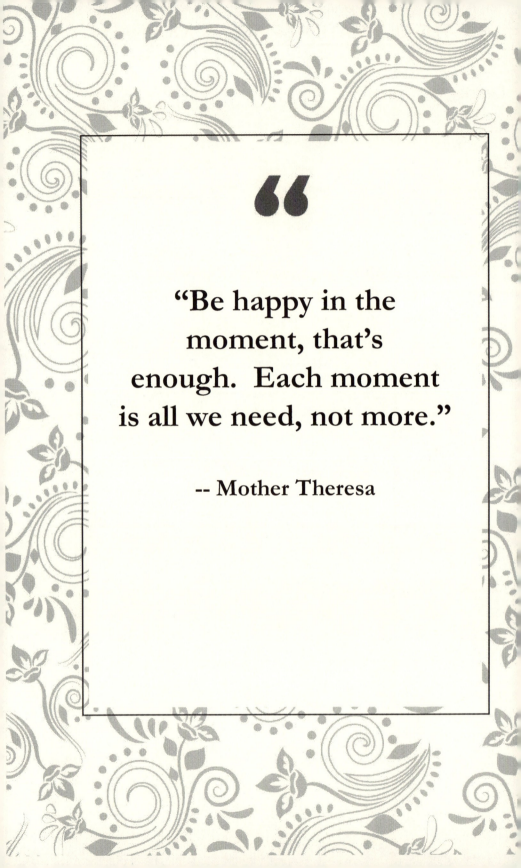

"Be happy in the moment, that's enough. Each moment is all we need, not more."

-- Mother Theresa

THE ULTIMATE HAPPINESS JOURNAL

Date: _____

Today's Happiest Moments:

_____
_____
_____

☐ Today I smiled at least once to a stranger.
☐ Today I did an intentional act of kindness.
☐ Today I spent at least 15+ minutes reading
inspirational content of my choice.

3 Things I'm Most Grateful For:

_____
_____
_____

What Could I Have Done Better?

_____
_____
_____

Goals/Plans for Tomorrow:

_____
_____
_____

Today's Great Accomplishments:

_____
_____
_____

How Happy Are You Feeling?　　☺　😐　☹

"

"Sometimes you need patience in order to find true happiness. It won't come fast. It won't be easy. But once you find it, it's worth it."

-- Unknown

THE ULTIMATE HAPPINESS JOURNAL

Date: _____

Today's Happiest Moments:

_____

_____

_____

☐ Today I smiled at least once to a stranger.
☐ Today I did an intentional act of kindness.
☐ Today I spent at least 15+ minutes reading
inspirational content of my choice.

3 Things I'm Most Grateful For:

_____

_____

_____

What Could I Have Done Better?

_____

_____

_____

Goals/Plans for Tomorrow:

_____

_____

_____

Today's Great Accomplishments:

_____

_____

_____

How Happy Are You Feeling?

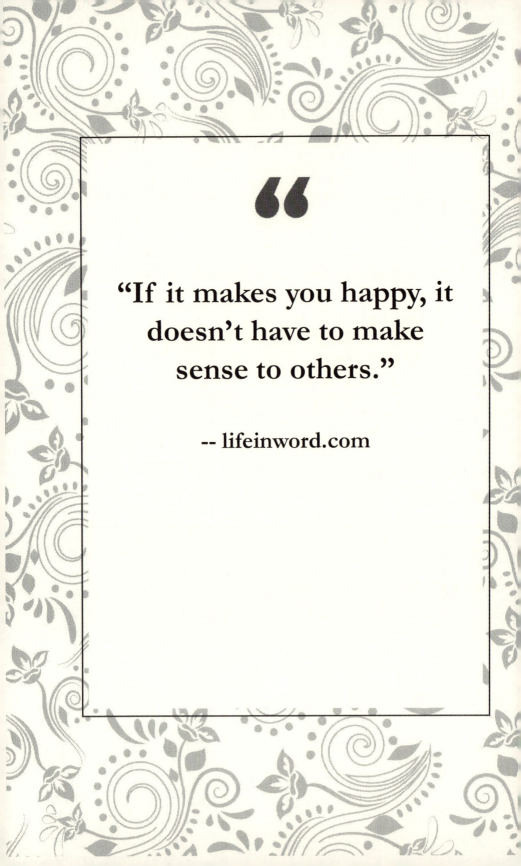

"If it makes you happy, it doesn't have to make sense to others."

-- lifeinword.com

THE ULTIMATE HAPPINESS JOURNAL

Date: _____

Today's Happiest Moments:

_____

_____

_____

☐ Today I smiled at least once to a stranger.
☐ Today I did an intentional act of kindness.
☐ Today I spent at least 15+ minutes reading inspirational content of my choice.

3 Things I'm Most Grateful For:

_____

_____

_____

What Could I Have Done Better?

_____

_____

_____

Goals/Plans for Tomorrow:

_____

_____

_____

Today's Great Accomplishments:

_____

_____

_____

How Happy Are You Feeling?   ☺ 😐 ☹

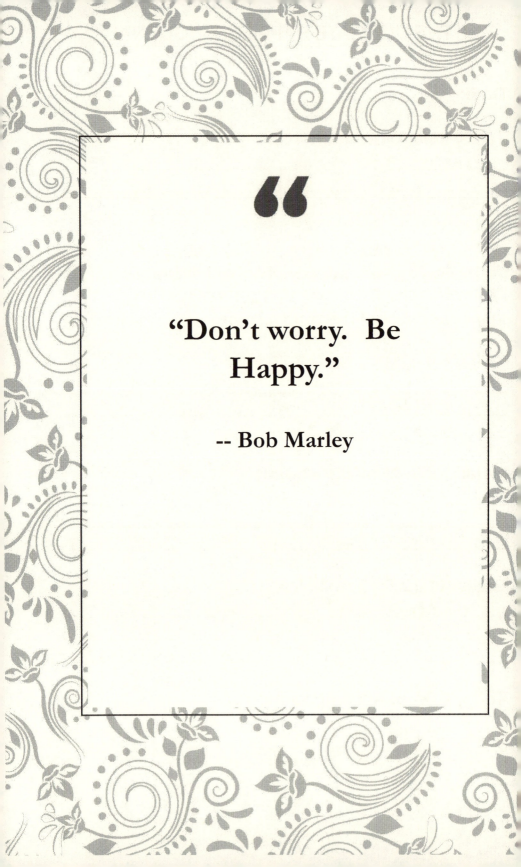

"Don't worry. Be Happy."

-- Bob Marley

THE ULTIMATE HAPPINESS JOURNAL

Date: _____

Today's Happiest Moments:

_____
_____
_____

☐ Today I smiled at least once to a stranger.
☐ Today I did an intentional act of kindness.
☐ Today I spent at least 15+ minutes reading
inspirational content of my choice.

3 Things I'm Most Grateful For:

_____
_____
_____

What Could I Have Done Better?

_____
_____
_____

Goals/Plans for Tomorrow:

_____
_____
_____

Today's Great Accomplishments:

_____
_____
_____

How Happy Are You Feeling?

"Happiness is in your ability to love others."

-- Leo Tolstoy

THE ULTIMATE HAPPINESS JOURNAL

Date: _____

Today's Happiest Moments:

_____

_____

_____

☐ Today I smiled at least once to a stranger.
☐ Today I did an intentional act of kindness.
☐ Today I spent at least 15+ minutes reading
inspirational content of my choice.

3 Things I'm Most Grateful For:

_____

_____

_____

What Could I Have Done Better?

_____

_____

_____

Goals/Plans for Tomorrow:

_____

_____

_____

Today's Great Accomplishments:

_____

_____

_____

How Happy Are You Feeling?   ☺   😐   ☹

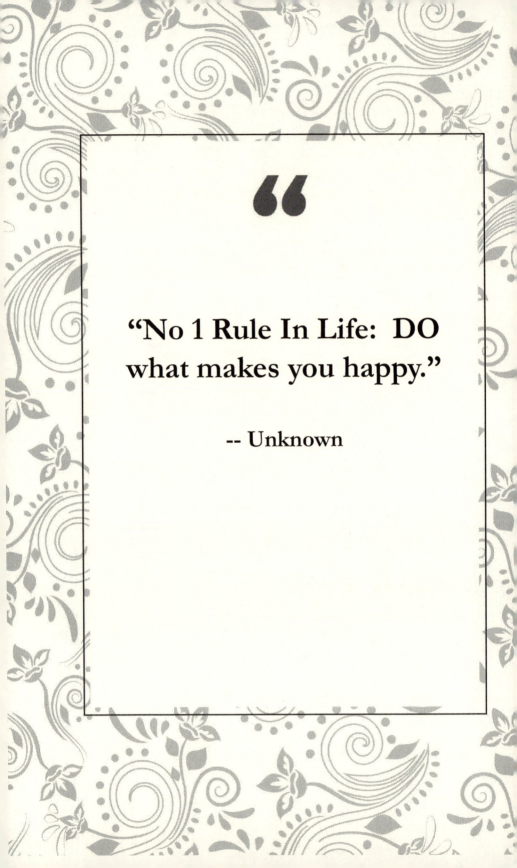

"No 1 Rule In Life: DO what makes you happy."

-- Unknown

THE ULTIMATE HAPPINESS JOURNAL

Date: _____

Today's Happiest Moments:

_____

_____

_____

☐ Today I smiled at least once to a stranger.
☐ Today I did an intentional act of kindness.
☐ Today I spent at least 15+ minutes reading
inspirational content of my choice.

3 Things I'm Most Grateful For:

_____

_____

_____

What Could I Have Done Better?

_____

_____

_____

Goals/Plans for Tomorrow:

_____

_____

_____

Today's Great Accomplishments:

_____

_____

_____

How Happy Are You Feeling?   ☺ ☻ ☹

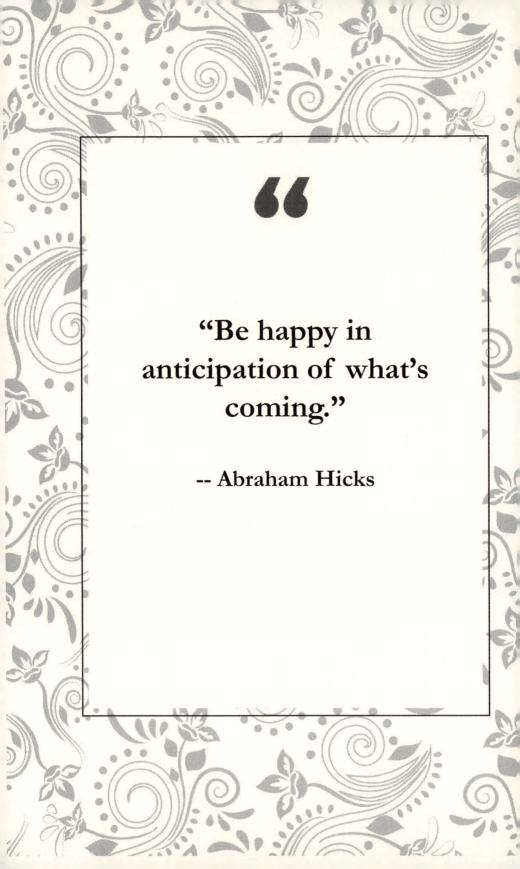

"Be happy in anticipation of what's coming."

-- Abraham Hicks

THE ULTIMATE HAPPINESS JOURNAL

Date: _____

Today's Happiest Moments:

_____
_____
_____

☐ Today I smiled at least once to a stranger.
☐ Today I did an intentional act of kindness.
☐ Today I spent at least 15+ minutes reading inspirational content of my choice.

3 Things I'm Most Grateful For:

_____
_____
_____

What Could I Have Done Better?

_____
_____
_____

Goals/Plans for Tomorrow:

_____
_____
_____

Today's Great Accomplishments:

_____
_____
_____

How Happy Are You Feeling?

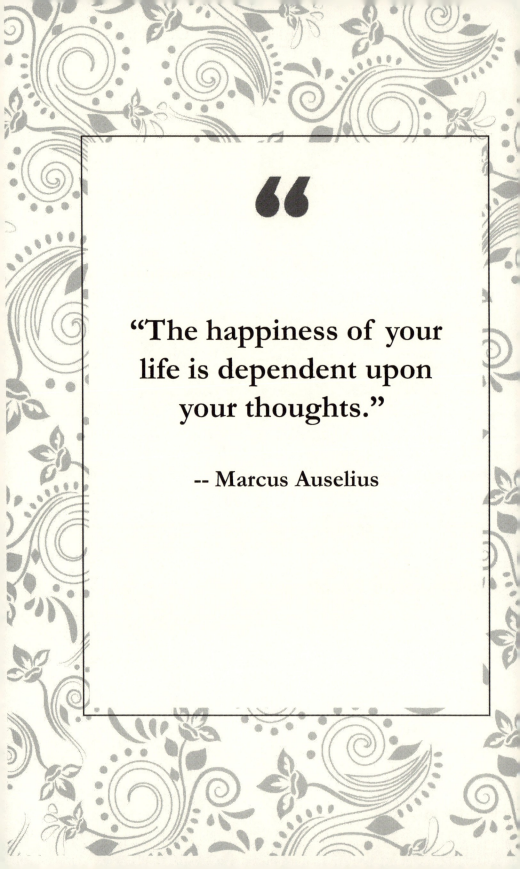

"The happiness of your life is dependent upon your thoughts."

-- Marcus Auselius

THE ULTIMATE HAPPINESS JOURNAL

Date: _____

Today's Happiest Moments:

_____

_____

_____

☐ Today I smiled at least once to a stranger.
☐ Today I did an intentional act of kindness.
☐ Today I spent at least 15+ minutes reading
inspirational content of my choice.

3 Things I'm Most Grateful For:

_____

_____

_____

What Could I Have Done Better?

_____

_____

_____

Goals/Plans for Tomorrow:

_____

_____

_____

Today's Great Accomplishments:

_____

_____

_____

How Happy Are You Feeling?   ☺   ☹   ☹

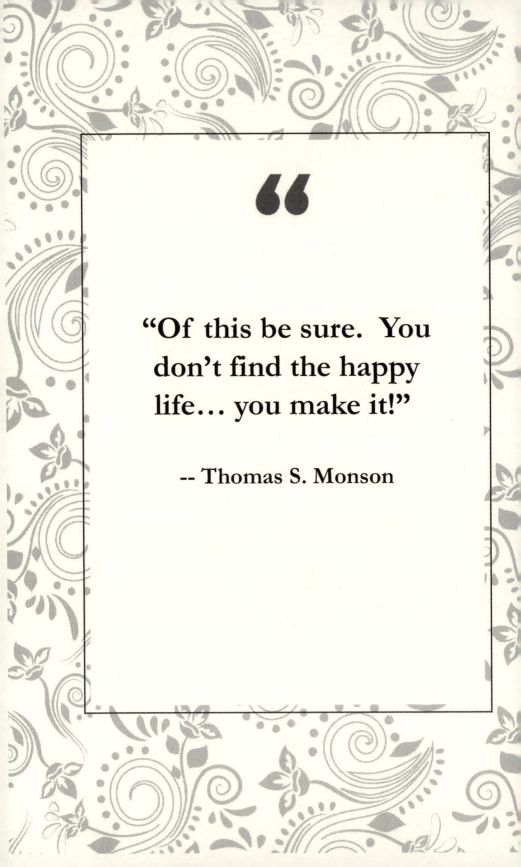

"Of this be sure. You don't find the happy life… you make it!"

-- Thomas S. Monson

THE ULTIMATE HAPPINESS JOURNAL

Date: _____

Today's Happiest Moments:

_____
_____
_____

☐ Today I smiled at least once to a stranger.
☐ Today I did an intentional act of kindness.
☐ Today I spent at least 15+ minutes reading
inspirational content of my choice.

3 Things I'm Most Grateful For:

_____
_____
_____

What Could I Have Done Better?

_____
_____
_____

Goals/Plans for Tomorrow:

_____
_____
_____

Today's Great Accomplishments:

_____
_____
_____

How Happy Are You Feeling?   ☺   😐   ☹

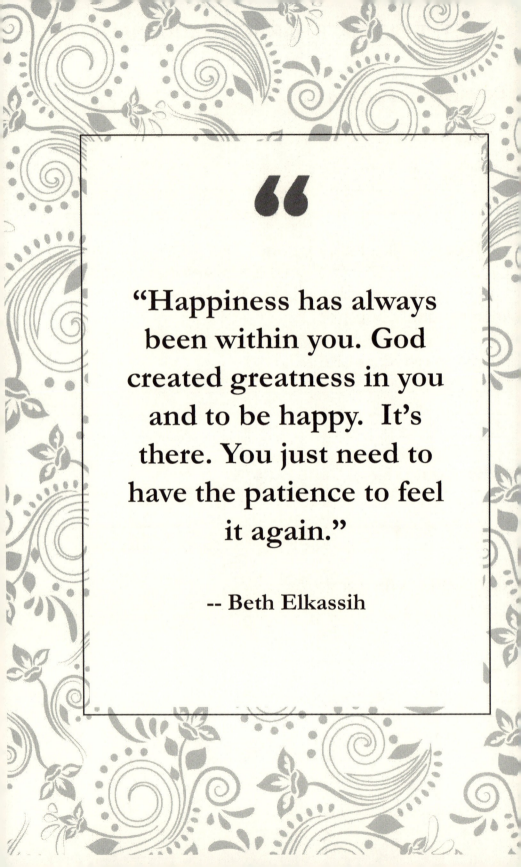

"Happiness has always
been within you. God
created greatness in you
and to be happy. It's
there. You just need to
have the patience to feel
it again."

-- Beth Elkassih

THE ULTIMATE HAPPINESS JOURNAL

Date: _____

Today's Happiest Moments:

_____

_____

_____

☐ Today I smiled at least once to a stranger.
☐ Today I did an intentional act of kindness.
☐ Today I spent at least 15+ minutes reading
inspirational content of my choice.

3 Things I'm Most Grateful For:

_____

_____

_____

What Could I Have Done Better?

_____

_____

_____

Goals/Plans for Tomorrow:

_____

_____

_____

Today's Great Accomplishments:

_____

_____

_____

How Happy Are You Feeling?   ☺ 😐 ☹

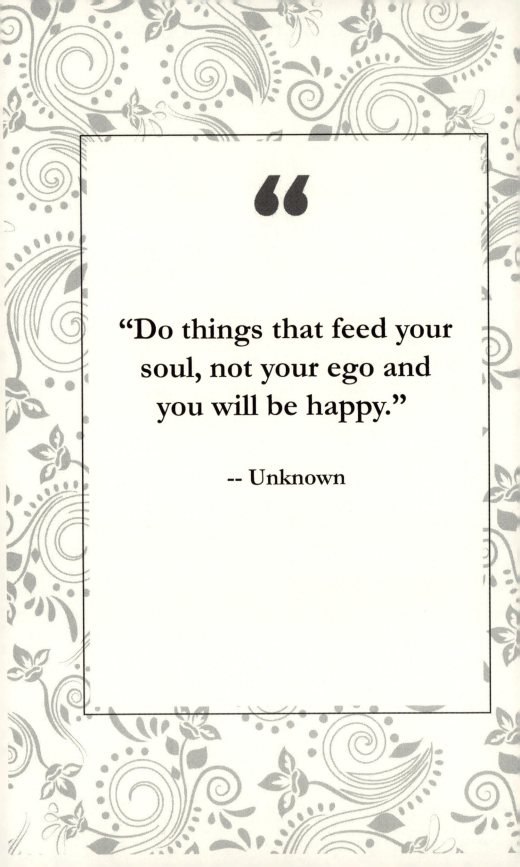

"

"Do things that feed your soul, not your ego and you will be happy."

-- Unknown

THE ULTIMATE HAPPINESS JOURNAL

Date: _____

Today's Happiest Moments:

_____
_____
_____

☐ Today I smiled at least once to a stranger.
☐ Today I did an intentional act of kindness.
☐ Today I spent at least 15+ minutes reading inspirational content of my choice.

3 Things I'm Most Grateful For:

_____
_____
_____

What Could I Have Done Better?

_____
_____
_____

Goals/Plans for Tomorrow:

_____
_____
_____

Today's Great Accomplishments:

_____
_____
_____

How Happy Are You Feeling?   ☺ 😐 ☹

"

"A secret to happiness is letting every situation be what it is instead of what you think it should be, and then making the best of it."

-- Unknown

THE ULTIMATE HAPPINESS JOURNAL

Date: _____

Today's Happiest Moments:

_____
_____
_____

☐ Today I smiled at least once to a stranger.
☐ Today I did an intentional act of kindness.
☐ Today I spent at least 15+ minutes reading
inspirational content of my choice.

3 Things I'm Most Grateful For:

_____
_____
_____

What Could I Have Done Better?

_____
_____
_____

Goals/Plans for Tomorrow:

_____
_____
_____

Today's Great Accomplishments:

_____
_____
_____

How Happy Are You Feeling?   ☺ ☻ ☹

"

"There are so many *beautiful* reasons to be happy."

-- Beth Elkassih

THE ULTIMATE HAPPINESS JOURNAL

Date: _____

Today's Happiest Moments:

_____

_____

_____

☐ Today I smiled at least once to a stranger.
☐ Today I did an intentional act of kindness.
☐ Today I spent at least 15+ minutes reading inspirational content of my choice.

3 Things I'm Most Grateful For:

_____

_____

_____

What Could I Have Done Better?

_____

_____

_____

Goals/Plans for Tomorrow:

_____

_____

_____

Today's Great Accomplishments:

_____

_____

_____

How Happy Are You Feeling?   ☺   😐   ☹

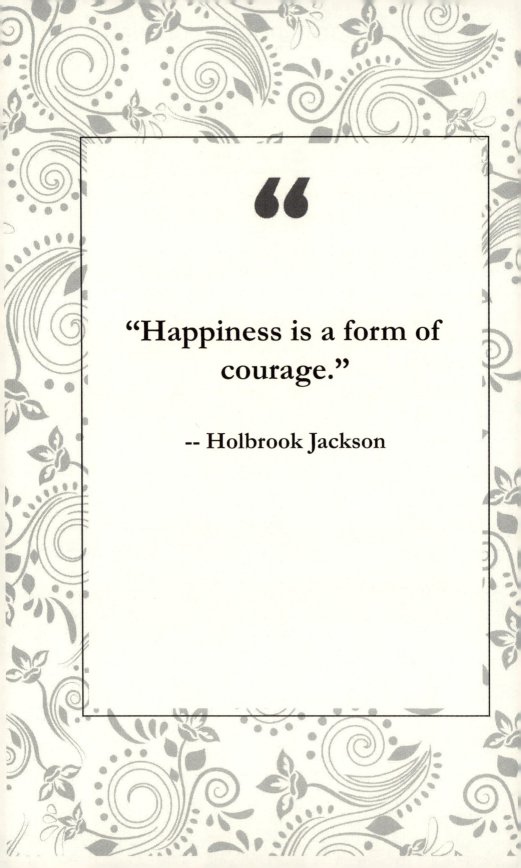

"Happiness is a form of courage."

-- Holbrook Jackson

THE ULTIMATE HAPPINESS JOURNAL

Date: _____

Today's Happiest Moments:

_____
_____
_____

☐ Today I smiled at least once to a stranger.
☐ Today I did an intentional act of kindness.
☐ Today I spent at least 15+ minutes reading
inspirational content of my choice.

3 Things I'm Most Grateful For:

_____
_____
_____

What Could I Have Done Better?

_____
_____
_____

Goals/Plans for Tomorrow:

_____
_____
_____

Today's Great Accomplishments:

_____
_____
_____

How Happy Are You Feeling?

"Happiness is where we find it, but rarely where we seek it."

-- J.Petit Sinn

THE ULTIMATE HAPPINESS JOURNAL

Date: _____

Today's Happiest Moments:

_____
_____
_____

☐ Today I smiled at least once to a stranger.
☐ Today I did an intentional act of kindness.
☐ Today I spent at least 15+ minutes reading inspirational content of my choice.

3 Things I'm Most Grateful For:

_____
_____
_____

What Could I Have Done Better?

_____
_____
_____

Goals/Plans for Tomorrow:

_____
_____
_____

Today's Great Accomplishments:

_____
_____
_____

How Happy Are You Feeling?   ☺ ☻ ☹

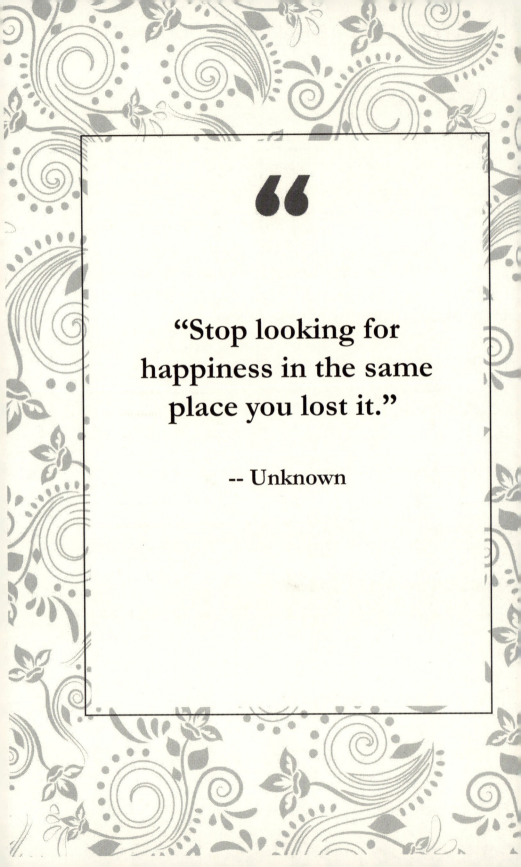

"Stop looking for happiness in the same place you lost it."

-- Unknown

THE ULTIMATE HAPPINESS JOURNAL

Date: _____

Today's Happiest Moments:

_____
_____
_____

☐ Today I smiled at least once to a stranger.
☐ Today I did an intentional act of kindness.
☐ Today I spent at least 15+ minutes reading
inspirational content of my choice.

3 Things I'm Most Grateful For:

_____
_____
_____

What Could I Have Done Better?

_____
_____
_____

Goals/Plans for Tomorrow:

_____
_____
_____

Today's Great Accomplishments:

_____
_____
_____

How Happy Are You Feeling?

"

"Nothing is impossible... even the word itself says 'I'm Possible!'"

-- Audrey Hepburn

THE ULTIMATE HAPPINESS JOURNAL

Date: _____

Today's Happiest Moments:

_____
_____
_____

☐ Today I smiled at least once to a stranger.
☐ Today I did an intentional act of kindness.
☐ Today I spent at least 15+ minutes reading
inspirational content of my choice.

3 Things I'm Most Grateful For:

_____
_____
_____

What Could I Have Done Better?

_____
_____
_____

Goals/Plans for Tomorrow:

_____
_____
_____

Today's Great Accomplishments:

_____
_____
_____

How Happy Are You Feeling?   ☺ 😐 ☹

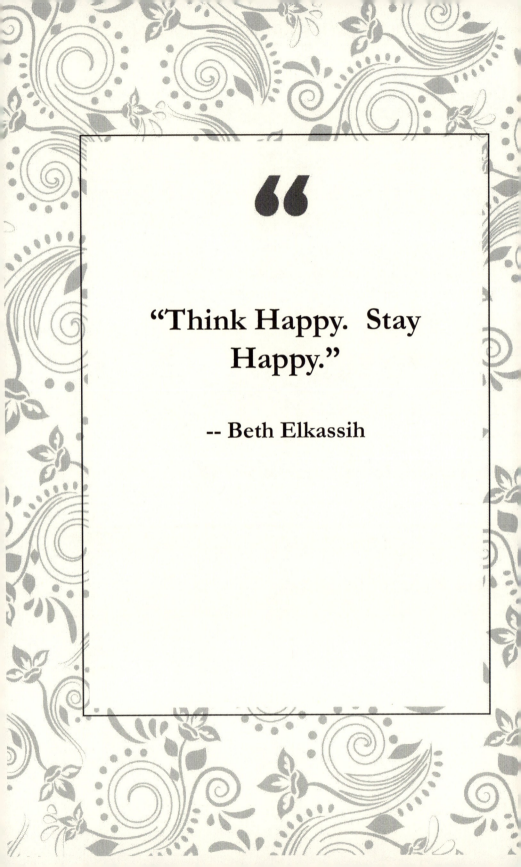

"Think Happy. Stay Happy."

-- Beth Elkassih

THE ULTIMATE HAPPINESS JOURNAL

Date: _____

Today's Happiest Moments:

_____

_____

_____

☐ Today I smiled at least once to a stranger.
☐ Today I did an intentional act of kindness.
☐ Today I spent at least 15+ minutes reading
inspirational content of my choice.

3 Things I'm Most Grateful For:

_____

_____

_____

What Could I Have Done Better?

_____

_____

_____

Goals/Plans for Tomorrow:

_____

_____

_____

Today's Great Accomplishments:

_____

_____

_____

How Happy Are You Feeling?

66

"Our days are happier
when we give people
a little bit of our
heart rather than
a piece of our
mind."

-- Unknown

THE ULTIMATE HAPPINESS JOURNAL

Date: _____

Today's Happiest Moments:

_____

_____

_____

☐ Today I smiled at least once to a stranger.
☐ Today I did an intentional act of kindness.
☐ Today I spent at least 15+ minutes reading
inspirational content of my choice.

3 Things I'm Most Grateful For:

_____

_____

_____

What Could I Have Done Better?

_____

_____

_____

Goals/Plans for Tomorrow:

_____

_____

_____

Today's Great Accomplishments:

_____

_____

_____

How Happy Are You Feeling?   ☺ 😐 ☹

66

"Healthiness is happiness."

-- Edward Diener

THE ULTIMATE HAPPINESS JOURNAL

Date: _____

Today's Happiest Moments:

_____
_____
_____

- ☐ Today I smiled at least once to a stranger.
- ☐ Today I did an intentional act of kindness.
- ☐ Today I spent at least 15+ minutes reading inspirational content of my choice.

3 Things I'm Most Grateful For:

_____
_____
_____

What Could I Have Done Better?

_____
_____
_____

Goals/Plans for Tomorrow:

_____
_____
_____

Today's Great Accomplishments:

_____
_____

How Happy Are You Feeling?

66

"You can never have too much 'happy'!

-- Beth Elkassih

THE ULTIMATE HAPPINESS JOURNAL

Date: _____

Today's Happiest Moments:

_____

_____

_____

☐ Today I smiled at least once to a stranger.
☐ Today I did an intentional act of kindness.
☐ Today I spent at least 15+ minutes reading
inspirational content of my choice.

3 Things I'm Most Grateful For:

_____

_____

_____

What Could I Have Done Better?

_____

_____

_____

Goals/Plans for Tomorrow:

_____

_____

_____

Today's Great Accomplishments:

_____

_____

_____

How Happy Are You Feeling?

"Keep calm and be happy, happy, happy."

-- Jeanine Aldridge

THE ULTIMATE HAPPINESS JOURNAL

Date: _____

Today's Happiest Moments:

_____
_____
_____

☐ Today I smiled at least once to a stranger.
☐ Today I did an intentional act of kindness.
☐ Today I spent at least 15+ minutes reading inspirational content of my choice.

3 Things I'm Most Grateful For:

_____
_____
_____

What Could I Have Done Better?

_____
_____
_____

Goals/Plans for Tomorrow:

_____
_____
_____

Today's Great Accomplishments:

_____
_____
_____

How Happy Are You Feeling?   ☺ 😐 ☹

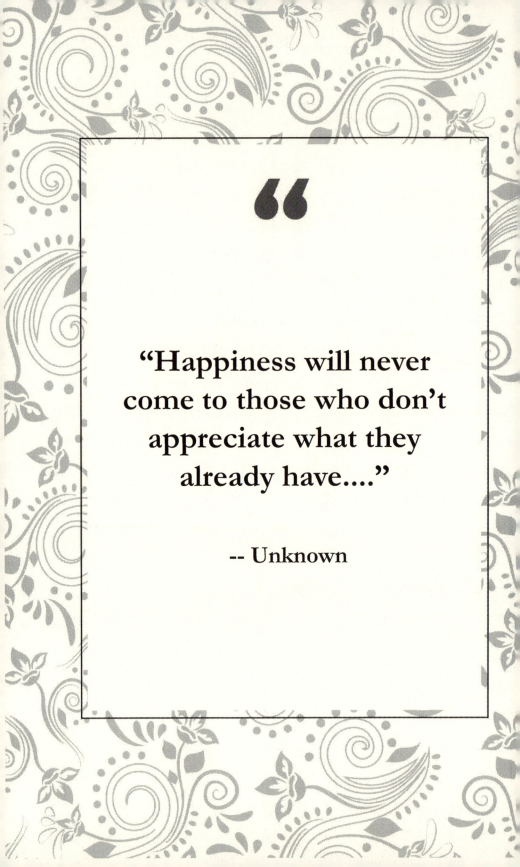

"Happiness will never come to those who don't appreciate what they already have...."

-- Unknown

THE ULTIMATE HAPPINESS JOURNAL

Date: _____

Today's Happiest Moments:

_____
_____
_____

☐ Today I smiled at least once to a stranger.
☐ Today I did an intentional act of kindness.
☐ Today I spent at least 15+ minutes reading
inspirational content of my choice.

3 Things I'm Most Grateful For:

_____
_____
_____

What Could I Have Done Better?

_____
_____
_____

Goals/Plans for Tomorrow:

_____
_____
_____

Today's Great Accomplishments:

_____
_____
_____

How Happy Are You Feeling?

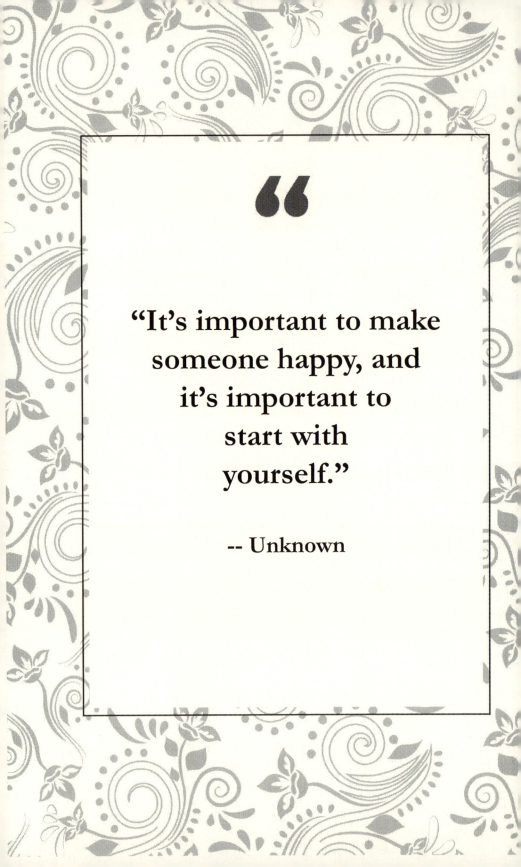

"It's important to make someone happy, and it's important to start with yourself."

-- Unknown

THE ULTIMATE HAPPINESS JOURNAL

Date: _____

Today's Happiest Moments:

_____
_____
_____

☐ Today I smiled at least once to a stranger.
☐ Today I did an intentional act of kindness.
☐ Today I spent at least 15+ minutes reading
inspirational content of my choice.

3 Things I'm Most Grateful For:

_____
_____
_____

What Could I Have Done Better?

_____
_____
_____

Goals/Plans for Tomorrow:

_____
_____
_____

Today's Great Accomplishments:

_____
_____
_____

How Happy Are You Feeling?   ☺ 😐 ☹

"

"Make today as beautiful as you can. Don't let anyone take your happiness away."

-- Beth Elkassih

THE ULTIMATE HAPPINESS JOURNAL

Date: _____

Today's Happiest Moments:

_____
_____
_____

☐ Today I smiled at least once to a stranger.
☐ Today I did an intentional act of kindness.
☐ Today I spent at least 15+ minutes reading
inspirational content of my choice.

3 Things I'm Most Grateful For:

_____
_____
_____

What Could I Have Done Better?

_____
_____
_____

Goals/Plans for Tomorrow:

_____
_____
_____

Today's Great Accomplishments:

_____
_____
_____

How Happy Are You Feeling?   ☺ ☺ ☹

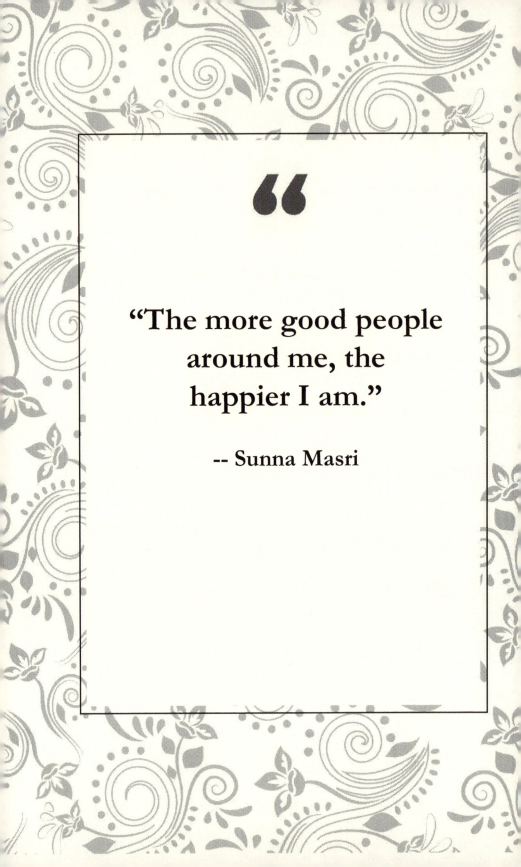

"The more good people around me, the happier I am."

-- Sunna Masri

THE ULTIMATE HAPPINESS JOURNAL

Date: _____

Today's Happiest Moments:

_____
_____
_____

☐ Today I smiled at least once to a stranger.
☐ Today I did an intentional act of kindness.
☐ Today I spent at least 15+ minutes reading inspirational content of my choice.

3 Things I'm Most Grateful For:

_____
_____
_____

What Could I Have Done Better?

_____
_____
_____

Goals/Plans for Tomorrow:

_____
_____
_____

Today's Great Accomplishments:

_____
_____
_____

How Happy Are You Feeling?

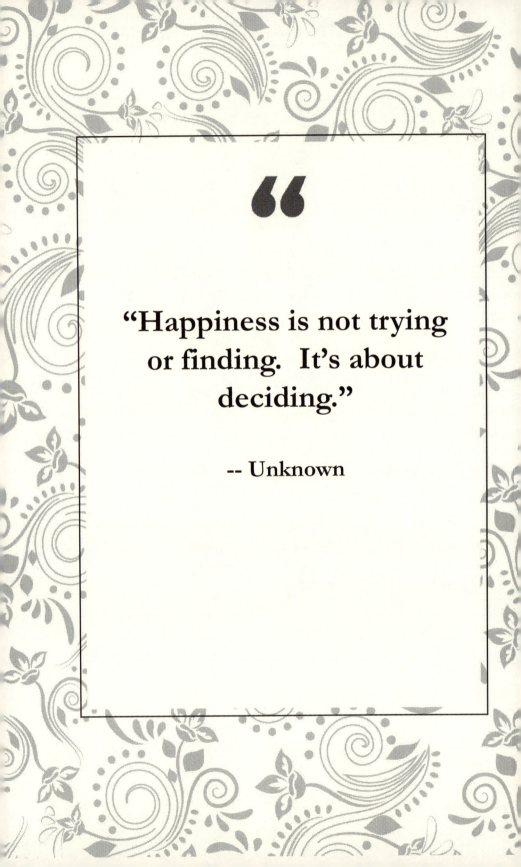

"Happiness is not trying or finding. It's about deciding."

-- Unknown

THE ULTIMATE HAPPINESS JOURNAL

Date: _____

Today's Happiest Moments:

_____
_____
_____

- ☐ Today I smiled at least once to a stranger.
- ☐ Today I did an intentional act of kindness.
- ☐ Today I spent at least 15+ minutes reading inspirational content of my choice.

3 Things I'm Most Grateful For:

_____
_____
_____

What Could I Have Done Better?

_____
_____
_____

Goals/Plans for Tomorrow:

_____
_____
_____

Today's Great Accomplishments:

_____
_____
_____

How Happy Are You Feeling?   ☺   😐   ☹

"

"Judge nothing and you
will be happy. Forgive
everything, you wlll
be happier. Love
everything, you will
be happiest."

-- Sri Chinmoy

THE ULTIMATE HAPPINESS JOURNAL

Date: _____

Today's Happiest Moments:

_____
_____
_____

- ☐ Today I smiled at least once to a stranger.
- ☐ Today I did an intentional act of kindness.
- ☐ Today I spent at least 15+ minutes reading inspirational content of my choice.

3 Things I'm Most Grateful For:

_____
_____
_____

What Could I Have Done Better?

_____
_____
_____

Goals/Plans for Tomorrow:

_____
_____
_____

Today's Great Accomplishments:

_____
_____
_____

How Happy Are You Feeling?   ☺ 😐 ☹

"The art of being happy lies in the power of extracting happiness from *common* things."

-- Henry Ward Beecher

THE ULTIMATE HAPPINESS JOURNAL

Date: _____

Today's Happiest Moments:

_____

_____

_____

☐ Today I smiled at least once to a stranger.
☐ Today I did an intentional act of kindness.
☐ Today I spent at least 15+ minutes reading
inspirational content of my choice.

3 Things I'm Most Grateful For:

_____

_____

_____

What Could I Have Done Better?

_____

_____

_____

Goals/Plans for Tomorrow:

_____

_____

_____

Today's Great Accomplishments:

_____

_____

_____

How Happy Are You Feeling?

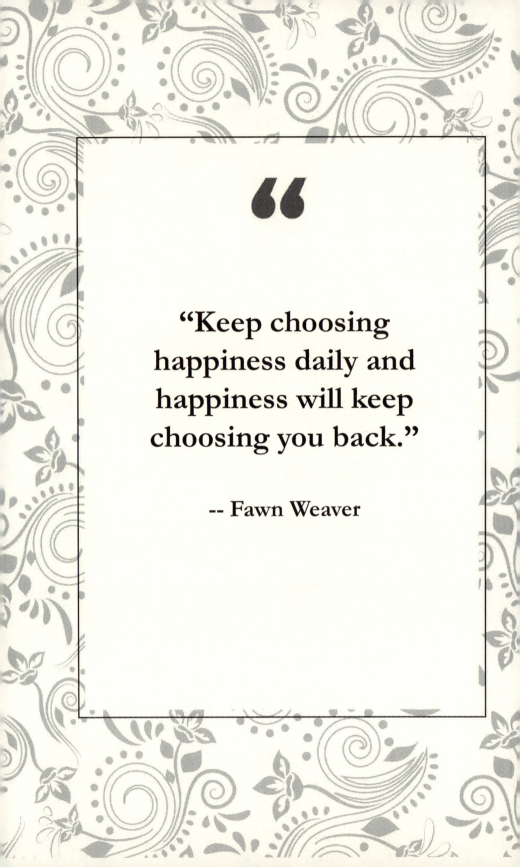

"

"Keep choosing happiness daily and happiness will keep choosing you back."

-- Fawn Weaver

60 DAY REFLECTIONS

Congratulations in completing the second 30 days of your 90-day Happiness journey. Let's take time out and reflect upon the past month.

How fulfilling has been the past 30 days/month?

_____
_____
_____

Did you achieve any of your weekly or monthly goals, and if so, what were they and what did you learn?

_____
_____
_____

Is there anything you would have done differently?

_____
_____
_____

What was the most enjoyable activity or activities you experienced these last 30 days?

_____
_____
_____

What is your most memorable 'act of kindness' you did for someone and one you received from someone?

_____
_____
_____

Name 3 Goals and/or Habits you wish to master for the next 30 days:

_____
_____
_____

"THE BAD NEWS:
There is no key
to happiness.
THE GOOD NEWS:
It isn't locked."

-- Unknown

THE ULTIMATE HAPPINESS JOURNAL

Date: _____

Today's Happiest Moments:

_____
_____
_____

- ☐ Today I smiled at least once to a stranger.
- ☐ Today I did an intentional act of kindness.
- ☐ Today I spent at least 15+ minutes reading inspirational content of my choice.

3 Things I'm Most Grateful For:

_____
_____
_____

What Could I Have Done Better?

_____
_____
_____

Goals/Plans for Tomorrow:

_____
_____
_____

Today's Great Accomplishments:

_____
_____
_____

How Happy Are You Feeling?

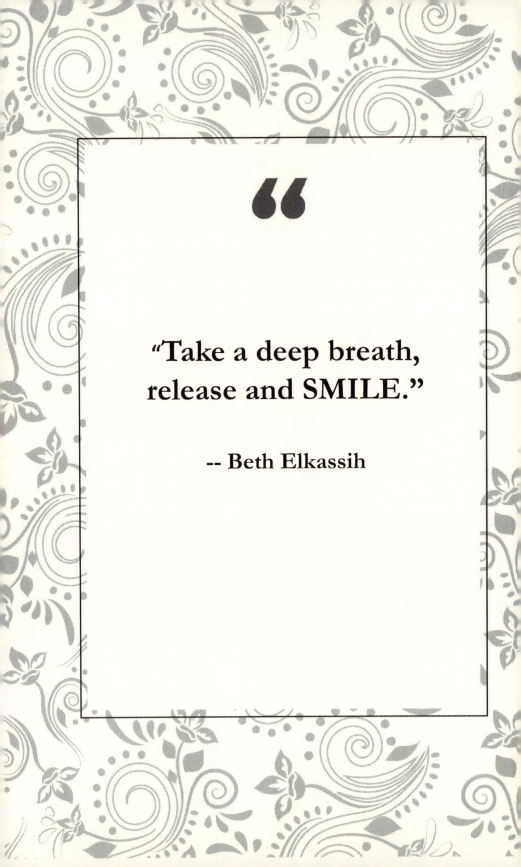

"

"Take a deep breath,
release and SMILE."

-- Beth Elkassih

THE ULTIMATE HAPPINESS JOURNAL

Date: _____

Today's Happiest Moments:

_____
_____
_____

☐ Today I smiled at least once to a stranger.
☐ Today I did an intentional act of kindness.
☐ Today I spent at least 15+ minutes reading
inspirational content of my choice.

3 Things I'm Most Grateful For:

_____
_____
_____

What Could I Have Done Better?

_____
_____
_____

Goals/Plans for Tomorrow:

_____
_____
_____

Today's Great Accomplishments:

_____
_____
_____

How Happy Are You Feeling?   ☺   😐   ☹

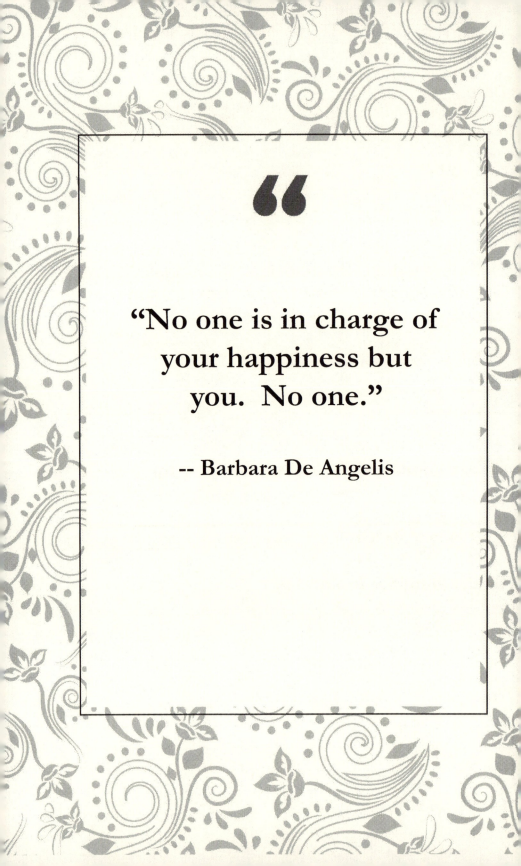

"

"No one is in charge of
your happiness but
you. No one."

-- Barbara De Angelis

THE ULTIMATE HAPPINESS JOURNAL

Date: _____

Today's Happiest Moments:

_____
_____
_____

☐ Today I smiled at least once to a stranger.
☐ Today I did an intentional act of kindness.
☐ Today I spent at least 15+ minutes reading
inspirational content of my choice.

3 Things I'm Most Grateful For:

_____
_____
_____

What Could I Have Done Better?

_____
_____
_____

Goals/Plans for Tomorrow:

_____
_____
_____

Today's Great Accomplishments:

_____
_____
_____

How Happy Are You Feeling? ☺ ☹ ☹

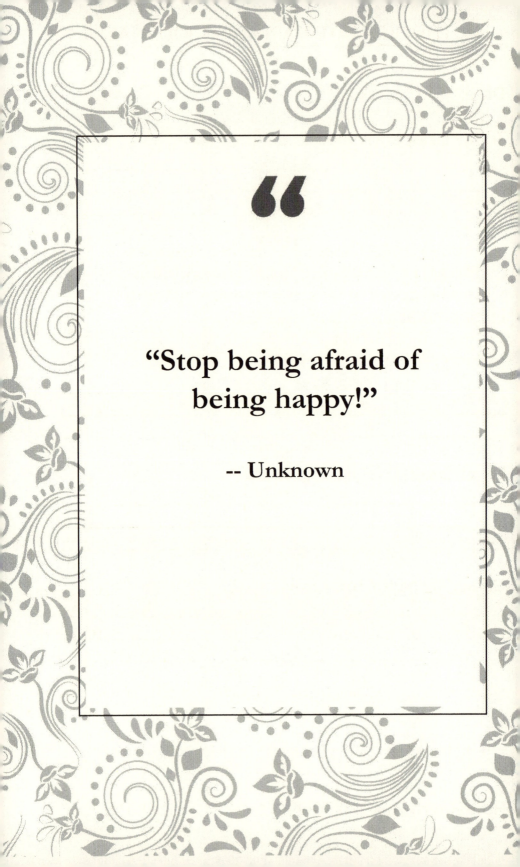

"Stop being afraid of being happy!"

-- Unknown

THE ULTIMATE HAPPINESS JOURNAL

Date: _____

Today's Happiest Moments:

_____
_____
_____

☐ Today I smiled at least once to a stranger.
☐ Today I did an intentional act of kindness.
☐ Today I spent at least 15+ minutes reading
inspirational content of my choice.

3 Things I'm Most Grateful For:

_____
_____
_____

What Could I Have Done Better?

_____
_____
_____

Goals/Plans for Tomorrow:

_____
_____
_____

Today's Great Accomplishments:

_____
_____
_____

How Happy Are You Feeling?   ☺   😐   ☹

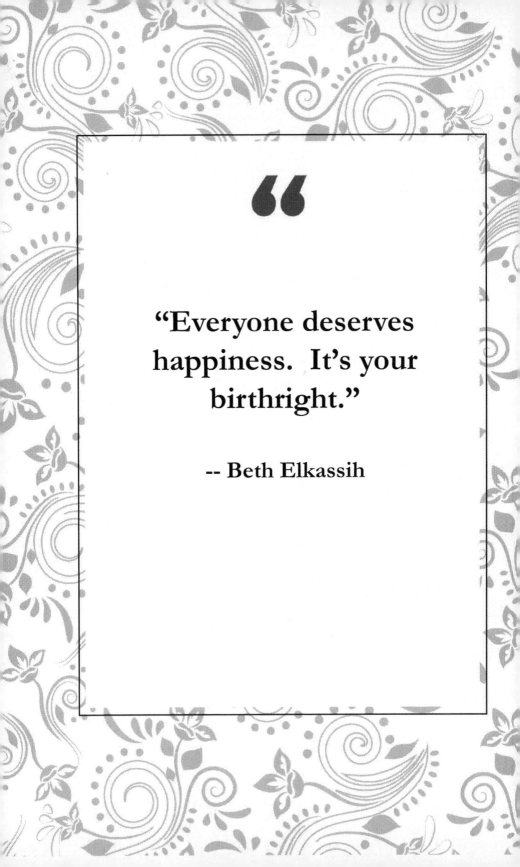

"Everyone deserves happiness. It's your birthright."

-- Beth Elkassih

THE ULTIMATE HAPPINESS JOURNAL

Date: _____

Today's Happiest Moments:

_____

_____

_____

☐ Today I smiled at least once to a stranger.
☐ Today I did an intentional act of kindness.
☐ Today I spent at least 15+ minutes reading
inspirational content of my choice.

3 Things I'm Most Grateful For:

_____

_____

_____

What Could I Have Done Better?

_____

_____

_____

Goals/Plans for Tomorrow:

_____

_____

_____

Today's Great Accomplishments:

_____

_____

_____

How Happy Are You Feeling?   ☺   😐   ☹

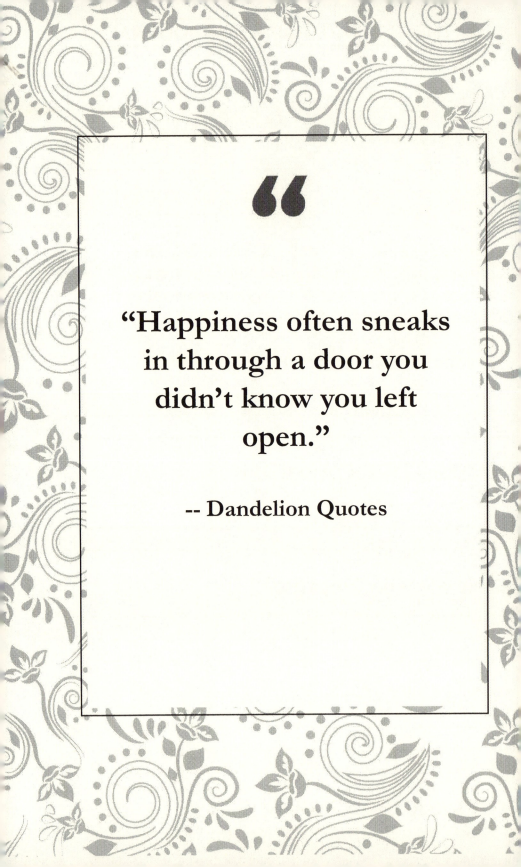

"

"Happiness often sneaks in through a door you didn't know you left open."

-- Dandelion Quotes

THE ULTIMATE HAPPINESS JOURNAL

Date: _____

Today's Happiest Moments:

_____
_____
_____

- [ ] Today I smiled at least once to a stranger.
- [ ] Today I did an intentional act of kindness.
- [ ] Today I spent at least 15+ minutes reading inspirational content of my choice.

3 Things I'm Most Grateful For:

_____
_____
_____

What Could I Have Done Better?

_____
_____
_____

Goals/Plans for Tomorrow:

_____
_____
_____

Today's Great Accomplishments:

_____
_____
_____

How Happy Are You Feeling?

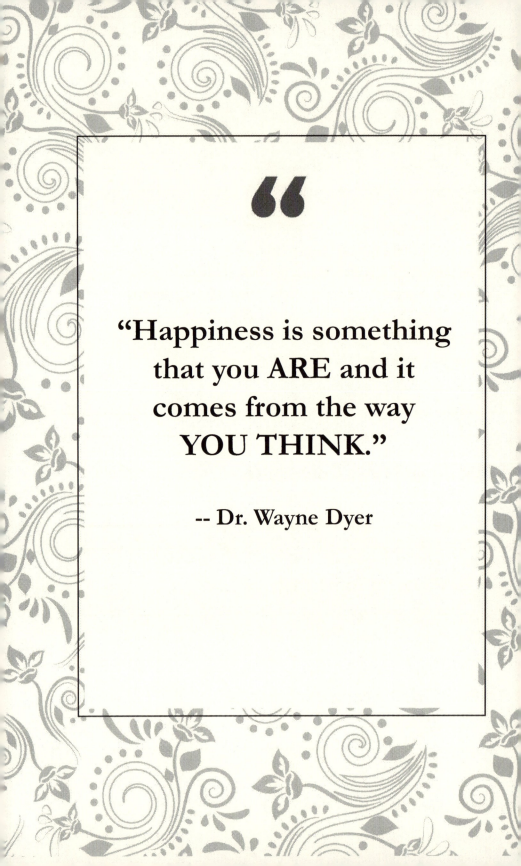

"

"Happiness is something that you **ARE** and it comes from the way **YOU THINK.**"

-- Dr. Wayne Dyer

THE ULTIMATE HAPPINESS JOURNAL

Date: _____

Today's Happiest Moments:

_____
_____
_____

☐ Today I smiled at least once to a stranger.
☐ Today I did an intentional act of kindness.
☐ Today I spent at least 15+ minutes reading
inspirational content of my choice.

3 Things I'm Most Grateful For:

_____
_____
_____

What Could I Have Done Better?

_____
_____
_____

Goals/Plans for Tomorrow:

_____
_____
_____

Today's Great Accomplishments:

_____
_____
_____

How Happy Are You Feeling?

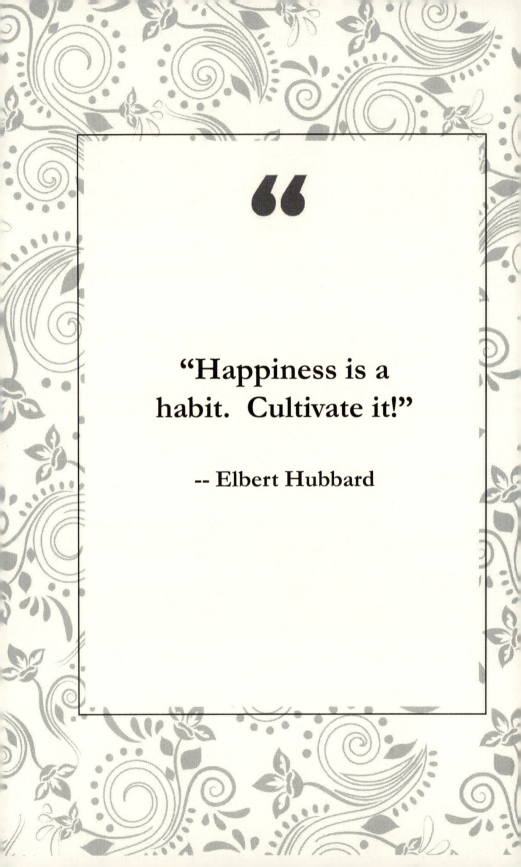

"

"Happiness is a
habit. Cultivate it!"

-- Elbert Hubbard

THE ULTIMATE HAPPINESS JOURNAL

Date: _____

Today's Happiest Moments:

_____
_____
_____

☐ Today I smiled at least once to a stranger.
☐ Today I did an intentional act of kindness.
☐ Today I spent at least 15+ minutes reading
inspirational content of my choice.

3 Things I'm Most Grateful For:

_____
_____
_____

What Could I Have Done Better?

_____
_____
_____

Goals/Plans for Tomorrow:

_____
_____
_____

Today's Great Accomplishments:

_____
_____
_____

How Happy Are You Feeling?

**"Happiness
and Gratitude
go
hand in hand."**

-- Beth Elkassih

THE ULTIMATE HAPPINESS JOURNAL

Date: _____

Today's Happiest Moments:

_____
_____
_____

- [ ] Today I smiled at least once to a stranger.
- [ ] Today I did an intentional act of kindness.
- [ ] Today I spent at least 15+ minutes reading inspirational content of my choice.

3 Things I'm Most Grateful For:

_____
_____
_____

What Could I Have Done Better?

_____
_____
_____

Goals/Plans for Tomorrow:

_____
_____
_____

Today's Great Accomplishments:

_____
_____
_____

How Happy Are You Feeling?   ☺ 😐 ☹

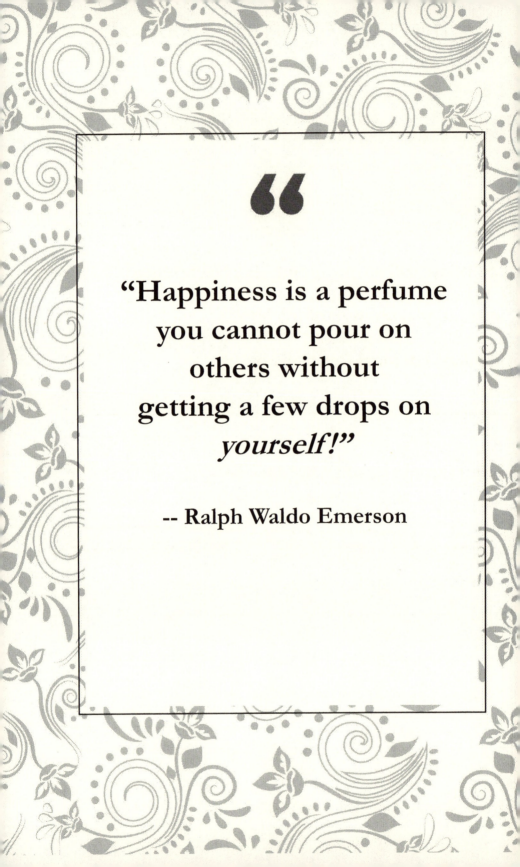

"

"Happiness is a perfume you cannot pour on others without getting a few drops on *yourself!*"

-- Ralph Waldo Emerson

THE ULTIMATE HAPPINESS JOURNAL

Date: _____

Today's Happiest Moments:

_____
_____
_____

☐ Today I smiled at least once to a stranger.
☐ Today I did an intentional act of kindness.
☐ Today I spent at least 15+ minutes reading inspirational content of my choice.

3 Things I'm Most Grateful For:

_____
_____
_____

What Could I Have Done Better?

_____
_____
_____

Goals/Plans for Tomorrow:

_____
_____
_____

Today's Great Accomplishments:

_____
_____
_____

How Happy Are You Feeling?   ☺ ☻ ☹

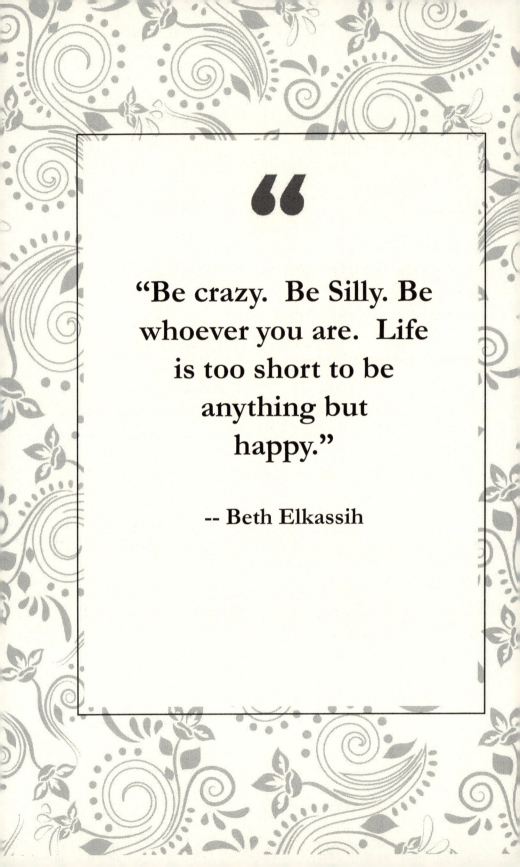

"**Be crazy. Be Silly. Be whoever you are. Life is too short to be anything but happy.**"

-- Beth Elkassih

THE ULTIMATE HAPPINESS JOURNAL

Date: _____

Today's Happiest Moments:

_____
_____
_____

☐ Today I smiled at least once to a stranger.
☐ Today I did an intentional act of kindness.
☐ Today I spent at least 15+ minutes reading
inspirational content of my choice.

3 Things I'm Most Grateful For:

_____
_____
_____

What Could I Have Done Better?

_____
_____
_____

Goals/Plans for Tomorrow:

_____
_____
_____

Today's Great Accomplishments:

_____
_____
_____

How Happy Are You Feeling?   ☺ ☺ ☹

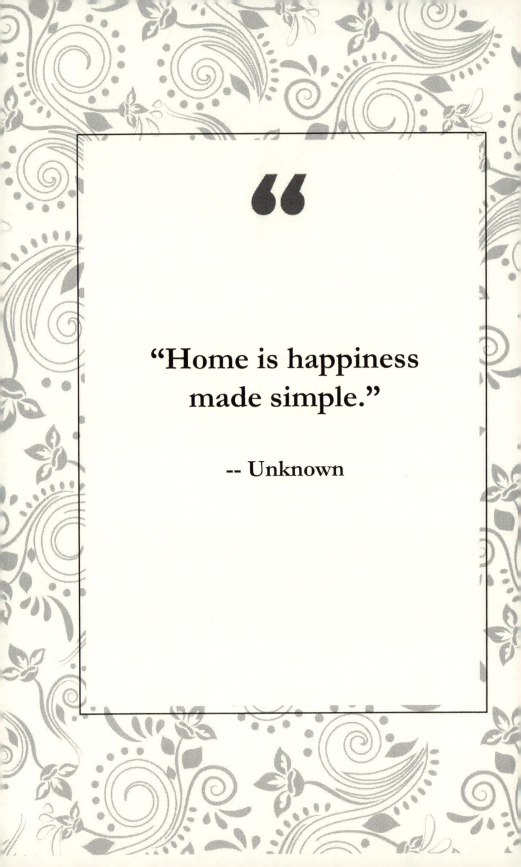

"

"Home is happiness
made simple."

-- Unknown

THE ULTIMATE HAPPINESS JOURNAL

Date: _____

Today's Happiest Moments:

_____

_____

_____

☐ Today I smiled at least once to a stranger.
☐ Today I did an intentional act of kindness.
☐ Today I spent at least 15+ minutes reading
inspirational content of my choice.

3 Things I'm Most Grateful For:

_____

_____

_____

What Could I Have Done Better?

_____

_____

_____

Goals/Plans for Tomorrow:

_____

_____

_____

Today's Great Accomplishments:

_____

_____

_____

How Happy Are You Feeling?   ☺ ☺ ☹

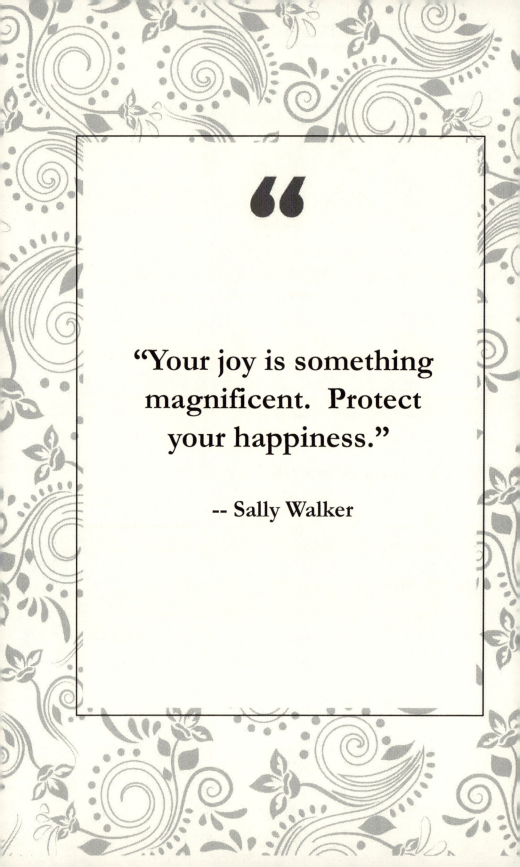

66

"Your joy is something magnificent. Protect your happiness."

-- Sally Walker

THE ULTIMATE HAPPINESS JOURNAL

Date: _____

Today's Happiest Moments:

_____
_____
_____

☐ Today I smiled at least once to a stranger.
☐ Today I did an intentional act of kindness.
☐ Today I spent at least 15+ minutes reading inspirational content of my choice.

3 Things I'm Most Grateful For:

_____
_____
_____

What Could I Have Done Better?

_____
_____
_____

Goals/Plans for Tomorrow:

_____
_____
_____

Today's Great Accomplishments:

_____
_____
_____

How Happy Are You Feeling?

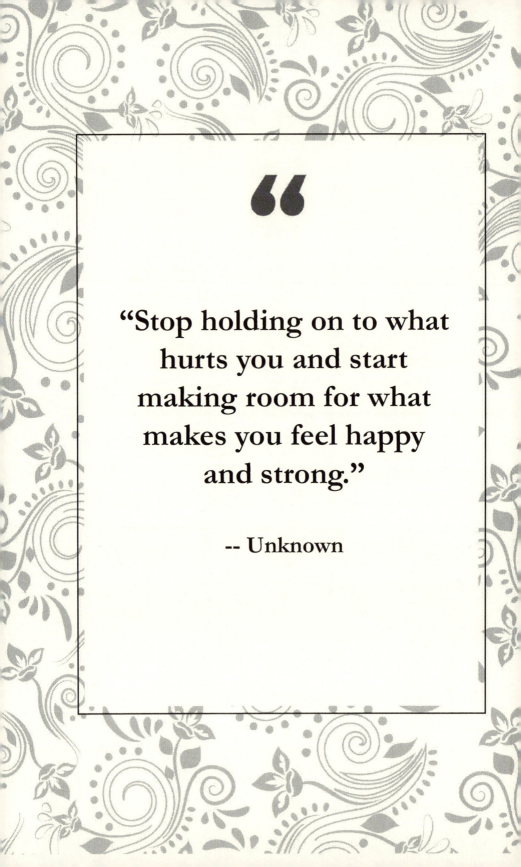

"Stop holding on to what hurts you and start making room for what makes you feel happy and strong."

-- Unknown

THE ULTIMATE HAPPINESS JOURNAL

Date: _____

Today's Happiest Moments:
_____
_____
_____

☐ Today I smiled at least once to a stranger.
☐ Today I did an intentional act of kindness.
☐ Today I spent at least 15+ minutes reading inspirational content of my choice.

3 Things I'm Most Grateful For:
_____
_____
_____

What Could I Have Done Better?
_____
_____
_____

Goals/Plans for Tomorrow:
_____
_____
_____

Today's Great Accomplishments:
_____
_____
_____

How Happy Are You Feeling?   ☺ 😐 ☹

"It's not selfish to love yourself, take care of yourself and to make your *happiness* a priority. It's necessary."

-- Mandy Hale

THE ULTIMATE HAPPINESS JOURNAL

Date: _____

Today's Happiest Moments:

_____
_____
_____

☐ Today I smiled at least once to a stranger.
☐ Today I did an intentional act of kindness.
☐ Today I spent at least 15+ minutes reading inspirational content of my choice.

3 Things I'm Most Grateful For:

_____
_____
_____

What Could I Have Done Better?

_____
_____
_____

Goals/Plans for Tomorrow:

_____
_____
_____

Today's Great Accomplishments:

_____
_____
_____

How Happy Are You Feeling?   ☺ ☺ ☹

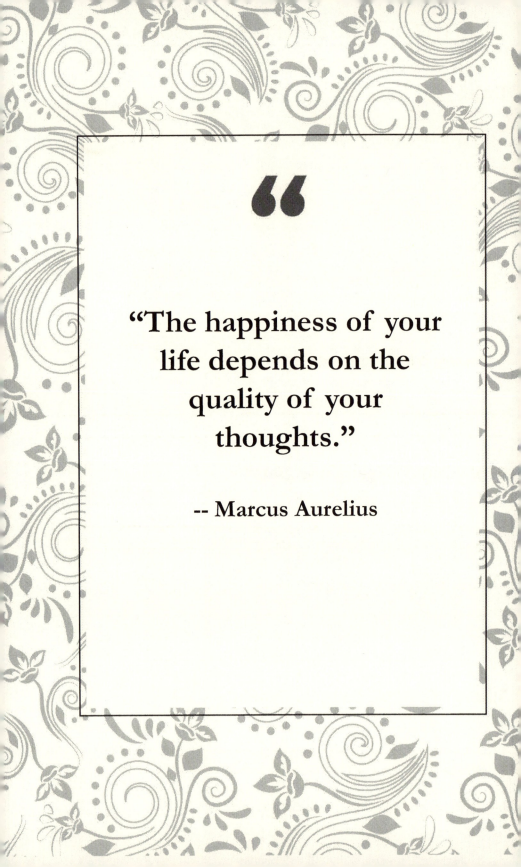

"The happiness of your life depends on the quality of your thoughts."

-- Marcus Aurelius

THE ULTIMATE HAPPINESS JOURNAL

Date: _____

Today's Happiest Moments:

_____
_____
_____

- ☐ Today I smiled at least once to a stranger.
- ☐ Today I did an intentional act of kindness.
- ☐ Today I spent at least 15+ minutes reading inspirational content of my choice.

3 Things I'm Most Grateful For:

_____
_____
_____

What Could I Have Done Better?

_____
_____
_____

Goals/Plans for Tomorrow:

_____
_____
_____

Today's Great Accomplishments:

_____
_____

How Happy Are You Feeling?   ☺   😐   ☹

"Happiness is more than doing fun things. Happiness is doing meaningful things."

-- Maxime Lagace

THE ULTIMATE HAPPINESS JOURNAL

Date: _____

Today's Happiest Moments:

_____
_____
_____

☐ Today I smiled at least once to a stranger.
☐ Today I did an intentional act of kindness.
☐ Today I spent at least 15+ minutes reading inspirational content of my choice.

3 Things I'm Most Grateful For:

_____
_____
_____

What Could I Have Done Better?

_____
_____
_____

Goals/Plans for Tomorrow:

_____
_____
_____

Today's Great Accomplishments:

_____
_____
_____

How Happy Are You Feeling?   ☺ ☻ ☹

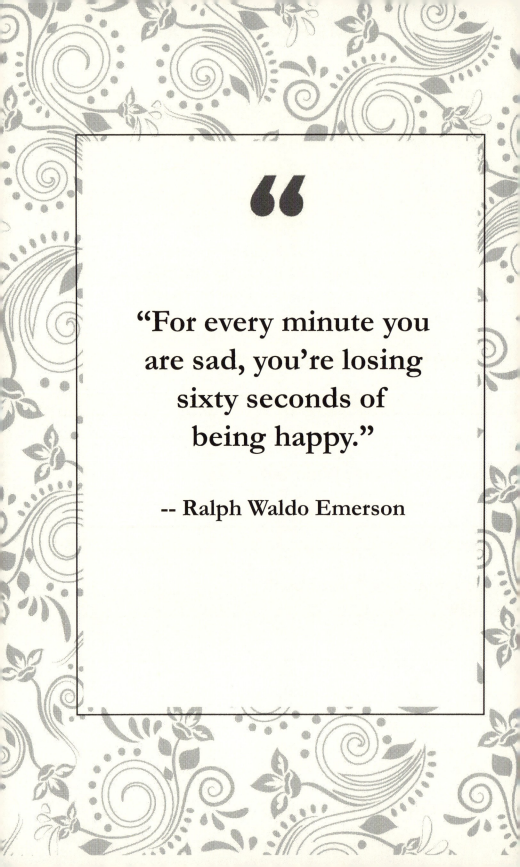

"For every minute you are sad, you're losing sixty seconds of being happy."

-- Ralph Waldo Emerson

THE ULTIMATE HAPPINESS JOURNAL

Date: _____

Today's Happiest Moments:

_____

_____

_____

☐ Today I smiled at least once to a stranger.
☐ Today I did an intentional act of kindness.
☐ Today I spent at least 15+ minutes reading
inspirational content of my choice.

3 Things I'm Most Grateful For:

_____

_____

_____

What Could I Have Done Better?

_____

_____

_____

Goals/Plans for Tomorrow:

_____

_____

_____

Today's Great Accomplishments:

_____

_____

_____

How Happy Are You Feeling?   ☺ 😐 ☹

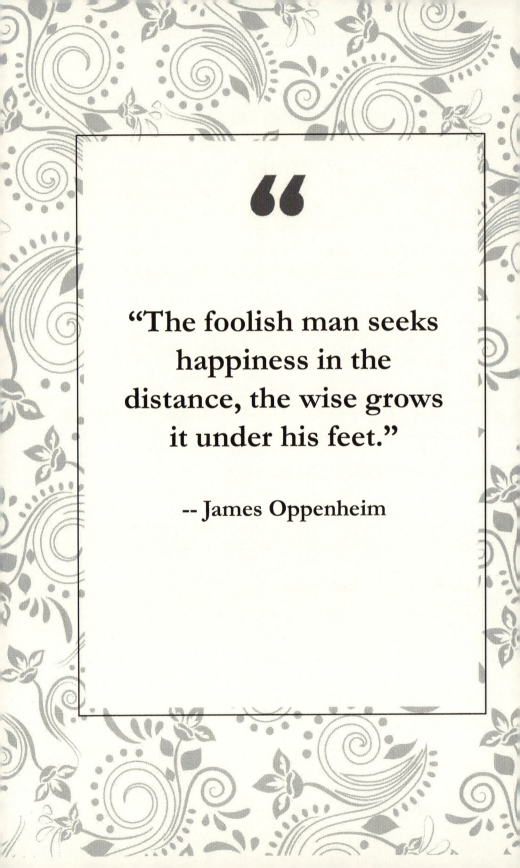

"The foolish man seeks happiness in the distance, the wise grows it under his feet."

-- James Oppenheim

THE ULTIMATE HAPPINESS JOURNAL

Date: _____

Today's Happiest Moments:

_____
_____
_____

☐ Today I smiled at least once to a stranger.
☐ Today I did an intentional act of kindness.
☐ Today I spent at least 15+ minutes reading inspirational content of my choice.

3 Things I'm Most Grateful For:

_____
_____
_____

What Could I Have Done Better?

_____
_____
_____

Goals/Plans for Tomorrow:

_____
_____
_____

Today's Great Accomplishments:

_____
_____
_____

How Happy Are You Feeling?

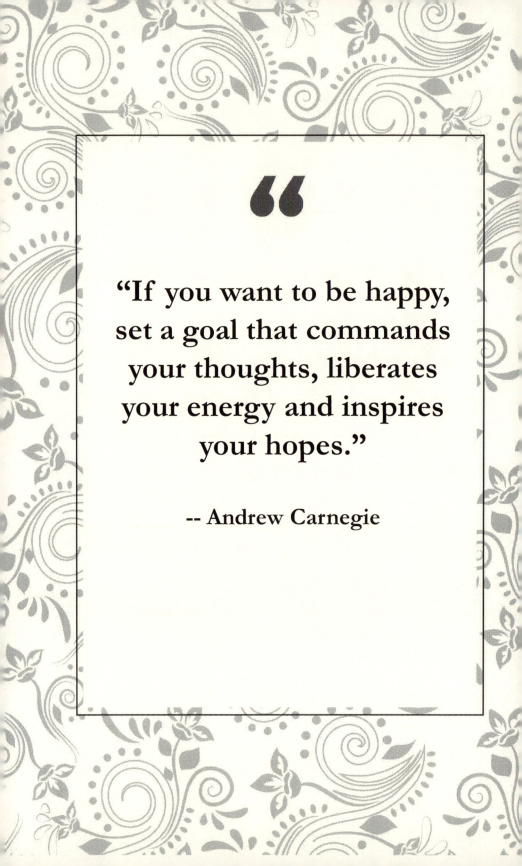

"If you want to be happy, set a goal that commands your thoughts, liberates your energy and inspires your hopes."

-- Andrew Carnegie

THE ULTIMATE HAPPINESS JOURNAL

Date: _____

Today's Happiest Moments:

_____

_____

_____

☐ Today I smiled at least once to a stranger.
☐ Today I did an intentional act of kindness.
☐ Today I spent at least 15+ minutes reading
inspirational content of my choice.

3 Things I'm Most Grateful For:

_____

_____

_____

What Could I Have Done Better?

_____

_____

_____

Goals/Plans for Tomorrow:

_____

_____

_____

Today's Great Accomplishments:

_____

_____

_____

How Happy Are You Feeling?

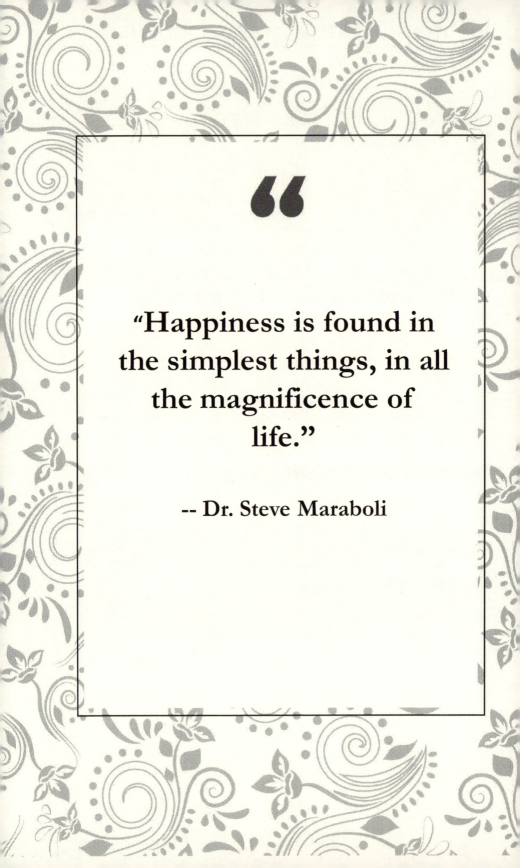

"Happiness is found in the simplest things, in all the magnificence of life."

-- Dr. Steve Maraboli

THE ULTIMATE HAPPINESS JOURNAL

Date: _____

Today's Happiest Moments:

_____

_____

_____

☐ Today I smiled at least once to a stranger.
☐ Today I did an intentional act of kindness.
☐ Today I spent at least 15+ minutes reading
inspirational content of my choice.

3 Things I'm Most Grateful For:

_____

_____

_____

What Could I Have Done Better?

_____

_____

_____

Goals/Plans for Tomorrow:

_____

_____

_____

Today's Great Accomplishments:

_____

_____

_____

How Happy Are You Feeling?

"Don't let silly little things steal your happiness."

-- Unknown

THE ULTIMATE HAPPINESS JOURNAL

Date: _____

Today's Happiest Moments:

_____

_____

_____

☐ Today I smiled at least once to a stranger.
☐ Today I did an intentional act of kindness.
☐ Today I spent at least 15+ minutes reading inspirational content of my choice.

3 Things I'm Most Grateful For:

_____

_____

_____

What Could I Have Done Better?

_____

_____

_____

Goals/Plans for Tomorrow:

_____

_____

_____

Today's Great Accomplishments:

_____

_____

_____

How Happy Are You Feeling?

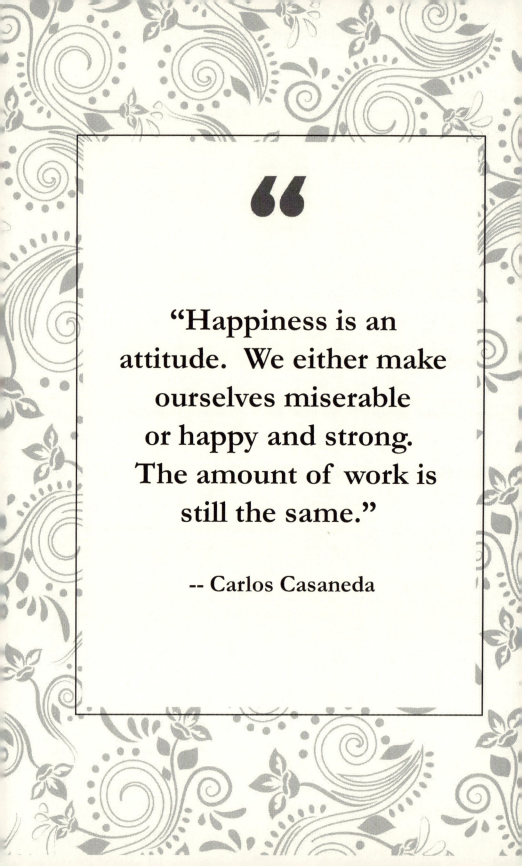

"

"Happiness is an
attitude. We either make
ourselves miserable
or happy and strong.
The amount of work is
still the same."

-- Carlos Casaneda

THE ULTIMATE HAPPINESS JOURNAL

Date: _____

Today's Happiest Moments:

_____
_____
_____

☐ Today I smiled at least once to a stranger.
☐ Today I did an intentional act of kindness.
☐ Today I spent at least 15+ minutes reading
inspirational content of my choice.

3 Things I'm Most Grateful For:

_____
_____
_____

What Could I Have Done Better?

_____
_____
_____

Goals/Plans for Tomorrow:

_____
_____
_____

Today's Great Accomplishments:

_____
_____
_____

How Happy Are You Feeling?

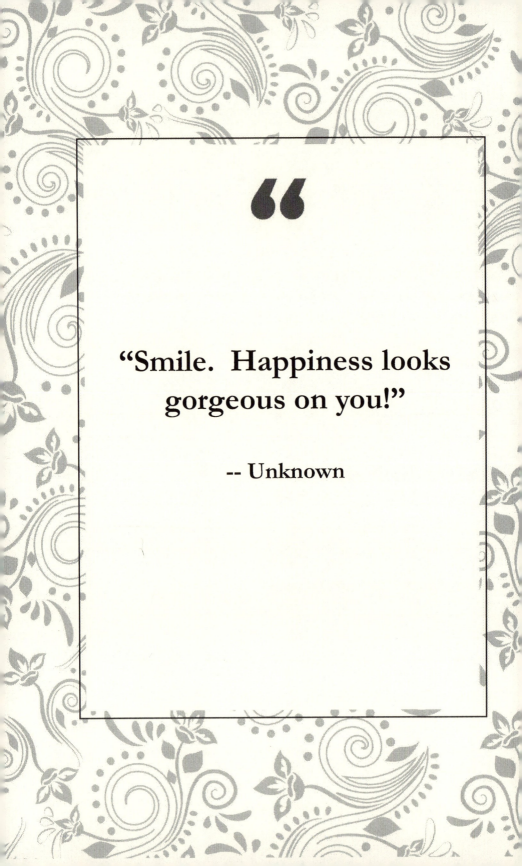

"Smile. Happiness looks gorgeous on you!"

-- Unknown

THE ULTIMATE HAPPINESS JOURNAL

Date: _____

Today's Happiest Moments:

_____
_____
_____

☐ Today I smiled at least once to a stranger.
☐ Today I did an intentional act of kindness.
☐ Today I spent at least 15+ minutes reading
inspirational content of my choice.

3 Things I'm Most Grateful For:

_____
_____
_____

What Could I Have Done Better?

_____
_____
_____

Goals/Plans for Tomorrow:

_____
_____
_____

Today's Great Accomplishments:

_____
_____
_____

How Happy Are You Feeling?

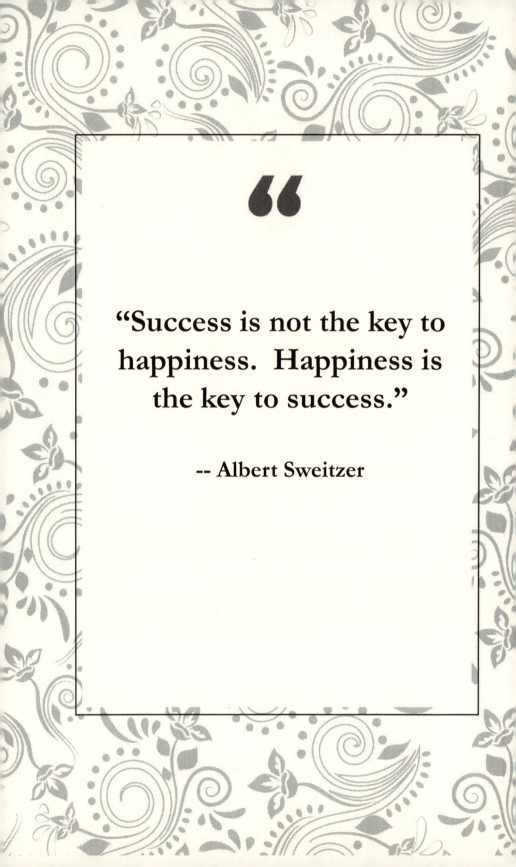

"Success is not the key to happiness. Happiness is the key to success."

-- Albert Sweitzer

THE ULTIMATE HAPPINESS JOURNAL

Date: _____

Today's Happiest Moments:

_____

_____

_____

☐ Today I smiled at least once to a stranger.
☐ Today I did an intentional act of kindness.
☐ Today I spent at least 15+ minutes reading
inspirational content of my choice.

3 Things I'm Most Grateful For:

_____

_____

_____

What Could I Have Done Better?

_____

_____

_____

Goals/Plans for Tomorrow:

_____

_____

_____

Today's Great Accomplishments:

_____

_____

_____

How Happy Are You Feeling?

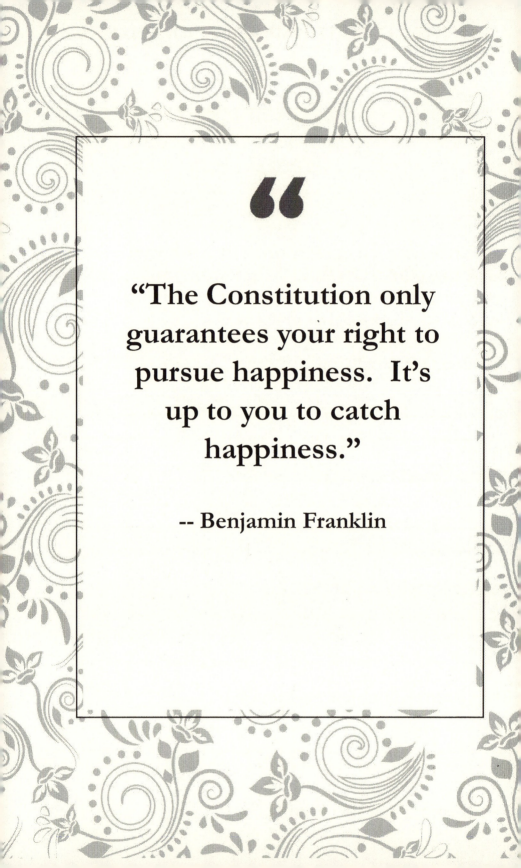

"

"The Constitution only guarantees your right to pursue happiness. It's up to you to catch happiness."

-- Benjamin Franklin

THE ULTIMATE HAPPINESS JOURNAL

Date: _____

Today's Happiest Moments:

_____

_____

_____

☐ Today I smiled at least once to a stranger.
☐ Today I did an intentional act of kindness.
☐ Today I spent at least 15+ minutes reading
inspirational content of my choice.

3 Things I'm Most Grateful For:

_____

_____

_____

What Could I Have Done Better?

_____

_____

_____

Goals/Plans for Tomorrow:

_____

_____

_____

Today's Great Accomplishments:

_____

_____

_____

How Happy Are You Feeling?

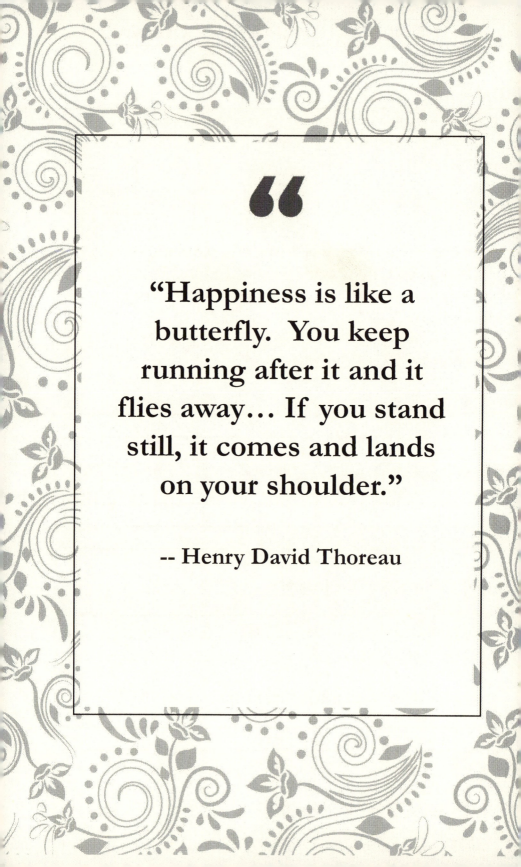

"

"Happiness is like a
butterfly. You keep
running after it and it
flies away… If you stand
still, it comes and lands
on your shoulder."

-- Henry David Thoreau

THE ULTIMATE HAPPINESS JOURNAL

Date: _____

Today's Happiest Moments:

_____
_____
_____

☐ Today I smiled at least once to a stranger.
☐ Today I did an intentional act of kindness.
☐ Today I spent at least 15+ minutes reading
inspirational content of my choice.

3 Things I'm Most Grateful For:

_____
_____
_____

What Could I Have Done Better?

_____
_____
_____

Goals/Plans for Tomorrow:

_____
_____
_____

Today's Great Accomplishments:

_____
_____

How Happy Are You Feeling?   ☺   ☺   ☹

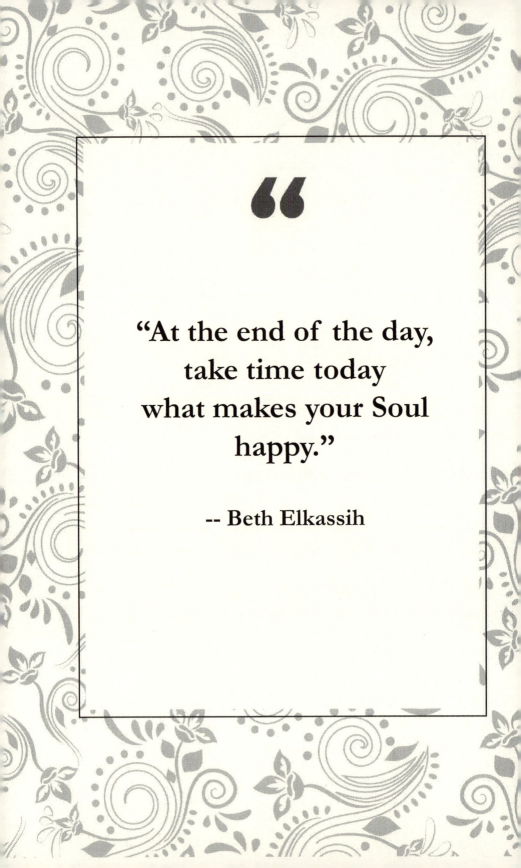

"

**"At the end of the day,
take time today
what makes your Soul
happy."**

-- Beth Elkassih

THE ULTIMATE HAPPINESS JOURNAL

Date: _____

Today's Happiest Moments:

_____
_____
_____

☐ Today I smiled at least once to a stranger.
☐ Today I did an intentional act of kindness.
☐ Today I spent at least 15+ minutes reading inspirational content of my choice.

3 Things I'm Most Grateful For:

_____
_____
_____

What Could I Have Done Better?

_____
_____
_____

Goals/Plans for Tomorrow:

_____
_____
_____

Today's Great Accomplishments:

_____
_____
_____

How Happy Are You Feeling?   ☺ 😐

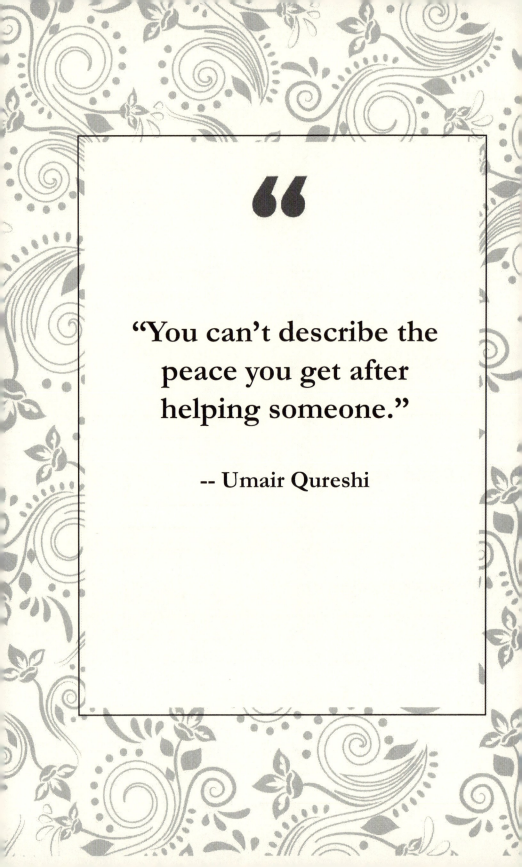

"You can't describe the peace you get after helping someone."

-- Umair Qureshi

THE ULTIMATE HAPPINESS JOURNAL

Date: _____

Today's Happiest Moments:

_____
_____
_____

☐ Today I smiled at least once to a stranger.
☐ Today I did an intentional act of kindness.
☐ Today I spent at least 15+ minutes reading
inspirational content of my choice.

3 Things I'm Most Grateful For:

_____
_____
_____

What Could I Have Done Better?

_____
_____
_____

Goals/Plans for Tomorrow:

_____
_____
_____

Today's Great Accomplishments:

_____
_____
_____

How Happy Are You Feeling?

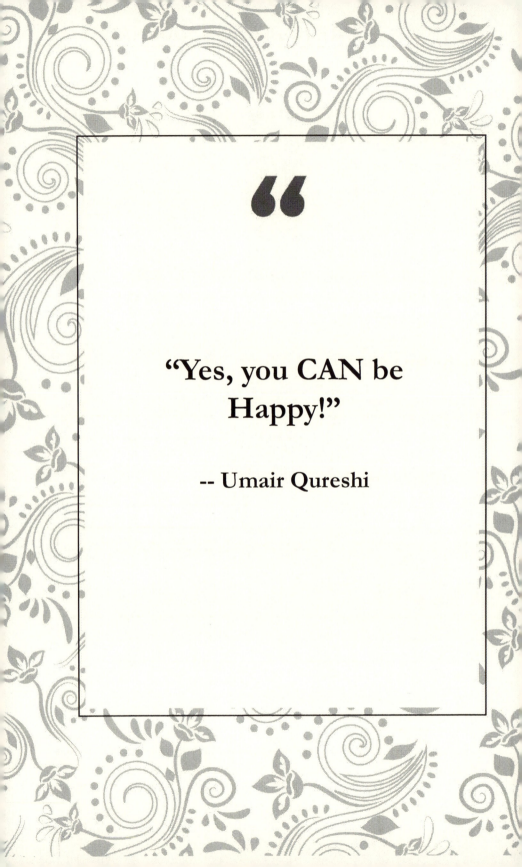

"Yes, you CAN be Happy!"

-- Umair Qureshi

THE ULTIMATE HAPPINESS JOURNAL

Date: _____

Today's Happiest Moments:

_____

_____

_____

☐ Today I smiled at least once to a stranger.
☐ Today I did an intentional act of kindness.
☐ Today I spent at least 15+ minutes reading
inspirational content of my choice.

3 Things I'm Most Grateful For:

_____

_____

_____

What Could I Have Done Better?

_____

_____

_____

Goals/Plans for Tomorrow:

_____

_____

_____

Today's Great Accomplishments:

_____

_____

_____

How Happy Are You Feeling?   ☹

"Don't forget to share the things you learned today."

-- Umair Qureshi

90 DAY REFLECTIONS

Congratulations in completing the third and final 30 days of your 90-day Happiness journey. Let's take time out and reflect upon the past month and 90 days..

How fulfilling has been the past 30 days/month?

_____

_____

_____

Did you achieve any of your weekly or monthly goals, and if so, what were they and what did you learn?

_____

_____

_____

Is there anything you would have done differently?

_____

_____

_____

What was the most enjoyable activity or activities you experienced these last 30 days?

_____

_____

_____

Has your level of Happiness increased significantly from when you started on this 90 day journey? What was your most significant 'take away' from this experience?

_____

_____

_____

_____

"Have some patience,
something bigger is
waiting for you!"

-- Umair Qureshi

Thank You for Completing this 90 Day Ultimate Happiness Journal!

We hope you loved this journal as much as we loved creating it for you. Reviews are always appreciated and you can either leave one on Amazon and/or you're more than welcome to leave a review and send to our email : *contact@zulzan.com*

Beth Jarboe-Elkassih is a professional Blogger of the website, *https://madeyousmileback.com* and also the author of "The Power of Unexpected Miracles", a book about 'Blessings in Disguise'. For more info, here is the link:
https://madeyousmileback.com/the-power-of-unexpected-miracles
It is offered in digital, paperback and audible formats.

Umair Qureshi is the Co-Founder of Zulzan LLC.
https://www.zulzan.com
Zulzan offers Creative Graphic Art Design, Web Development and Mobile Apps.

ADDITIONAL NOTES

_____

_____

_____

_____

_____

_____

_____

_____

_____

_____

_____

_____

_____

_____

ADDITIONAL NOTES

_____

_____

_____

_____

_____

_____

_____

_____

_____

_____

_____

_____

_____

ADDITIONAL NOTES

ADDITIONAL NOTES

_____

_____

_____

_____

_____

_____

_____

_____

_____

_____

_____

_____

_____

_____

ADDITIONAL NOTES

_____

_____

_____

_____

_____

_____

_____

_____

_____

_____

_____

_____

_____

_____

ADDITIONAL NOTES

_____

_____

_____

_____

_____

_____

_____

_____

_____

_____

_____

_____

_____

_____

_____

ADDITIONAL NOTES

_____

_____

_____

_____

_____

_____

_____

_____

_____

_____

_____

_____

_____

_____

Made in the USA
Middletown, DE
10 January 2020

82998874R00120